PORCELLIAN CLUB CENTENNIAL 1791-1891

PORCELLIAN CLUB CENTENNIAL

1791-1891

KALPAZ

ISBN: 978-93-5128-763-6

First Published in 1891
Indian Reprint in 2017

Published by

Kalpaz Publications
C-30, Satyawati Nagar,
Delhi – 110052
E-mail: kalpaz@hotmail.com
Website: kalpazpublications.com
Ph.: +91-9212142040

PREFATORY

The new building which, at the meeting held in February, 1890, it was decided to erect has been completed, and is now occupied by the Club. During the period of construction, temporary quarters were secured at 414 Harvard Street. The new building stands upon the site of the old building which the Club had occupied since the year 1833. In order to celebrate in an appropriate manner the completion of the work and the Centennial Anniversary of the Founding of the Porcellian Club, a committee, consisting of the Building Committee and the officers of the Club, was chosen. February 21, 1891, was selected as the date, and it was decided to have the Annual Meeting and certain Literary Exercises commemorative of the occasion precede the Dinner. The Committee has prepared this volume containing the Literary Exercises, a brief account of the Dinner, and a catalogue of the members of the Club to date. A full account of the Annual Meeting and the Dinner may be found in the Club records.

The thanks of the Committee and of the Club are due to Brothers Honorary Sargent, Isham, and Chapman for their contribution towards the success of the Literary Exercises; also to Brother Honorary Hazeltine for his interest in preparing the plates for the memorial programme; also to Brother Honorary Painter for revising the Club Catalogue.

GEO. B. SHATTUCK, '63,
F. R. APPLETON, '75,
R. M. SALTONSTALL, '80,
G. P. UPHAM, JR., '81,
W. C. BAYLIES, '84,
A. T. FRENCH, '85,
N. LONGWORTH, '91,
L. BROOKS, '91,
S. T. CHASE, '92,
} *Committee on Anniversary.*

PORCELLIAN CLUB, CAMBRIDGE, *May* 1, 1891.

CONTENTS

CATALOGUE

LIST OF ILLUSTRATIONS

PORCELLIAN CLUB

CENTENNIAL CELEBRATION

FOUNDED 1791

"by the light of the Moon."

Cambridge

· 1891 ·

PROGRAMME.

BUILDING OPEN FOR INSPECTION,

3.00 P.M.

BUSINESS MEETING,

4.30 P.M.

LITERARY EXERCISES,

5.00 P.M.

I. INITIATION OF NEW MEMBERS, N. LONGWORTH, '91, D. M'l.

II. SONG. Written for the Club in '46, By Bro. Hon. O. W. HOLMES, '29.

Bro. Hon. WISTER, '82, Chorister.

III. HISTORY OF THE CLUB, ... Bro. Hon. ISHAM, '76.

IV. "DUM VIVIMUS VIVAMUS," . By Bro. Hon. WISTER, '82, Chorister.

V. ODE, ... Bro. Hon. J. O. SARGENT, 30.

VI. POEM, ... Bro. Hon. H. G. CHAPMAN, '83.

VII. THE CLUB SONG, ... Chorister.

"FEBRUARY SUPPER."

7.00 P.M.

A SONG OF OTHER DAYS.

As o'er the glacier's frozen sheet
  Breathes soft the Alpine rose,
So, through life's desert springing sweet,
  The flower of friendship grows;
And as, where'er the roses grow,
  Some rain or dew descends,
'Tis nature's law that wine should flow
  To wet the lips of friends.
    Then once again, before we part,
      My empty glass shall ring;
    And he that has the warmest heart
      Shall loudest laugh and sing.

They say we were not born to eat;
  But gray-haired sages think
It means, — Be moderate in your meat,
  And partly live to drink;
For baser tribes the rivers flow
  That know not wine or song;
Man wants but little drink below,
  But wants that little strong.
    Then once again, etc.

If one bright drop is like the gem
  That decks a monarch's crown,
One goblet holds a diadem
  Of rubies melted down!
A fig for Cæsar's blazing brow,
  But, like the Egyptian queen,
Bid each dissolving jewel glow
  My thirsty lips between.
    Then once again, etc.

The Grecian's mound, the Roman's urn,
  Are silent when we call,
Yet still the purple grapes return
  To cluster on the wall;
It was a bright Immortal's head
  They circled with the vine,
And o'er their best and bravest dead
  They poured the dark-red wine.
    Then once again, etc.

Methinks o'er every sparkling glass
  Young Eros waves his wings.
And echoes o'er its dimples pass
  From dead Anacreon's strings;
And, tossing round its beaded brim
  Their locks of floating gold,
With bacchant dance and choral hymn
  Return the nymphs of old.
    Then once again, etc.

A welcome then to joy and mirth,
  From hearts as fresh as ours,
To scatter o'er the dust of earth
  Their sweetly mingled flowers;
'T is Wisdom's self the cup that fills
  In spite of Folly's frown,
And Nature, from her vine-clad hills,
  That rains her life-blood down!
    Then once again, before we part,
      My empty glass shall ring;
    And he that has the warmest heart
      Shall loudest laugh and sing.

"DUM VIVIMUS VIVAMUS."

I.

In old days of glory —
So I have heard the story —
When true hearts were many
  And false hearts were few,
Libations crowned with flowers
They poured out to the powers,
To bless their mortal hours
  Each day anew.

II.

But we need no roses,
The wine to us discloses
A flower more precious
  That blooms in the bowl.
And no man e'er shall blame us
That brothers here we name us:
Dum vivimus vivamus
  With heart and soul.

III.

When these days are no longer
Our memory 'll grow the stronger,
To it we shall hearken
  As through the world we roll;
Its voice we cannot smother,
And when we meet a brother
We'll drink to one another
  With heart and soul.

FIDE ET AMICITIA
DUM VIVIMUS VIVAMUS

HISTORY OF THE CLUB

BY BRO. HON. CHARLES ISHAM, '76

BROTHER GRAND AND BROTHERS:

The Porcellian Club, as it flourishes to-day, is the rare survival of generous sentiments, so personal in their nature that they might seem of necessity confined to the lives of contemporaries, and to be of a delicacy incapable of transmission in their purity throughout the changes of a century.

Yet, knowing that we have received these excellent gifts, unimpaired and ever fresh from the hearts of our predecessors, we may learn from our records that not to chance or to the infusion of any alloy is due their abundant vitality among us.

In the year 1789, and doubtless for some time previously, there existed in Harvard College an organization called by its members *The Argonauts*, and sufficiently formal to meet every alternate week for the enjoyment of an impromptu supper. A former historian of the Club, who, presumably, was himself an argonaut, has left us an elaborate essay to prove that the lineal descendants of Jason's companions were then to be found in Cambridge rather than in Colchis; but there is evidence that his argument was not intended to be convincing, and we certainly are more fortunate in the character of Joseph McKean, who in 1791 entered the College, and was almost immediately received into this band of Grecians.

"To be famous when one is young," it has been said, "is the privilege of the gods," and surely no youth of whom the Harvard Annals tell us united in juster proportion the qualities of manliness and amiability that inspired our Honored Founder. How quickly and willingly his influence was recognized is shown by his creation of this Fraternity, under the title of "The Pig Club," in the year 1791, when it fell to him in turn to offer an entertainment to *The Argonauts*, at which he presided and furnished the table with a young pig, roasted whole, that he had with infinite dexterity concealed in his room until it was fit to sacrifice upon the altar of Conviviality. Some of the votes, though none of the records, of "The Pig Club" have come down to us. If ever written, they were probably few in number, since, in the course of the following year, the name was changed to that of "The Gentleman's Society," and, at the same time, a Grand Marshal and a Deputy were elected from the Senior Class and a Corresponding and Recording Secretary from the Juniors, individually and collectively to exercise their authority in accordance with a set of rules, exceedingly brief, and introduced by a preamble, explaining that, "Whereas the multiplication of laws tends to weaken their force, we, despising the metaphysics which teach that the principles of order and good nature are not innate, and proposing by our future actions to demonstrate that they are, leave the regulation of his conduct to the good sense of each individual."

Joseph McKean, being ineligible for the higher offices, was made the Secretary, and Charles Cutler the Grand Marshal. The latter resigned upon graduation; and the former thereupon succeeded him, continuing preëminently influential in shaping the brilliant Destiny of the Club until 1798, when he declined reëlection, having ordered its Government, determined its Policy, and imbued it with his personality, as we believe, for many hundred years.

During the administration of Joseph McKean, it was resolved that thereafter the Grand Marshal should be chosen from among the Graduate Honoraries. Immediate membership was confined to the three upper classes. Sociability, Brotherly Affection and Generosity, Liberality and Courtesy, were invoked as our principles; and, to disarm mistaken criticism, it was voted, in July of 1794, "that this Fraternity be denominated the Porcellian Club," and that a silver seal, still in our archives, be struck to commemorate a name long to be held in dignity and honor.

Our affectionate admiration could dwell on the commanding physique and intellectual graces of our Founder, or recount his daring yet innocent escapades. He was truly the embodiment of strength and activity and of refined and wholesome mirth, opposed to license and to every form of over indulgence. Within two years after he had quitted the Grand Marshal's chair he received the tribute of a toast, familiar to all Porcellians, and his gracious figure appeared at the Anniversary table in 1805 to invoke a benediction; for, following the dictates of his conscience and humanity, he had become a minister of the Congregational church.

But it remains to indicate how well his successors understood the importance of adhering to the standard of his work; nor was this accomplished without trial. Indeed, before our Fraternity was forty years old, the Brothers had not merely rejected a series of propositions insidiously calculated to rob us of our distinction, but they had also confirmed the original, simple purpose in a manner to withstand all later and harmful attempts at innovation.

The members assembled in each other's rooms for private

entertainments and the unaffected play of wit and kindly feeling. The Secretary had the custody of the Club property, and in his room meetings for the transaction of business were generally held in response to notices posted on the door of the College Chapel. Public festivities, in the sense that the Public witnessed the procession of Porcellians from the room used as a rendezvous to the place of entertainment, were voted from time to time, and a preference was shown for the resources of Porter's Tavern in Brighton Street, just out of Harvard Square.

The Anniversary Meeting was presently set for the day of the Autumnal Exhibition, when a Grand Marshal was chosen from the Fraternity at large, and on the second Thursday in June members were elected from the Sophomore Class, and a Deputy from the Juniors. In February of the year 1800, it was moved and carried that some badge be designed "expressive of Unanimity, Liberality, and Friendship;" and before the end of the month the heart-shaped medal was adopted, to be worn suspended from the neck by ribbons of green and white, the colors to be replaced by black should Death enter the circle of the Brothers Immediate.

At the beginning of the century the Club possessed some fourscore Brothers Honorary. Already the interest and enjoyment of all stated meetings was rated in proportion to their attendance. Happily, they resided, with scarcely an exception, in Boston or in the vicinity of Cambridge, and were thus enabled to take part frequently in the pleasantest reunions, and to gratify a desire to share the intimacy of their most recent exponents. Had the question been asked then, or were it to be asked now, To what circumstance, above all others, should be attributed the prosperity, and, perhaps, the existence, of the Club?

the answer would have been, and is, To the sympathy and coöperation of the Honorary Members, to their prudent advice and their ready generosity. In a thousand ways they have invited and retained the confidence of their younger Brethren, and the attachments of both, inextricably knit around the parent stock, are the pledges of its continuing vigor and beauty.

The first mention of a book, the property of the Club, relates to a "Musical miscellany for the encouragement of Vocalists." A desire to form a library had, however, previously been expressed, and in April, 1803, it was formally begun with Brother Samuel Kirkland's presentation of Young's "Travels in France" and Cowper's "Task." The Librarianship was to be held by a Senior, and Joseph Sprague was first chosen to this most responsible office.

At its inception the Library increased by gifts, averaging fifty volumes a year. It contains at present over ten thousand books, and is exceedingly valuable from its many handsome specimens of printing and binding, yet, especially, as a monument of instinctive preference in every department of Literature. The first catalogue was published in 1816, and successive editions have marked the growth of the collection. The majority of our by-laws relate to the use and maintenance of the Library; and the small membership of the Club has proved an important factor of constant gains and comparatively inconsiderable losses.

In the minutes of our business meetings we trace the suppression of tendencies peculiar to society in general one hundred years ago, but gradually perceived to form no part of our identity. A certain ostentation we once shared with the world around us. The badge of the Club was much oftener worn, and Porcellian processions, headed by music, marched to points remote to dine and return with the same or greater ceremony. The efforts of the members to secure a local habitation were hastened through their inclination for less publicity; and, when once enjoying their own room, processions soon ceased, and as early as 1821 further decoration than the medal was prohibited, and the occasions considered proper for its display were carefully limited.

The incompatibility of chapters, dependent on a club absolutely identified with its surroundings and the individuality of its members, did not prevent a serious discussion of this matter in "the Thirties," when a zeal for extension prevailed among Greek-letter societies. The temptation was, however, overcome by the reflection that concentration was of the essence of the Club Spirit, although others might imitate our example in the hope of increasing the measure of their happiness. On the other hand, several college organizations of the Past, before deciding in the negative the significant question, "Is life worth living?" have confided to our keeping their papers and relics, thus securing for themselves a posthumous immortality.

The reinforcement of the Club by the admission of "The Knights of the Square Table," in 1831, was a fortunate conjunction, because the objects of each were similar, and the membership of both had well-nigh converged.

The Committee on behalf of the Porcellians invited complete amalgamation, on condition that their title be accepted to include the Knights; and this having been agreed to, the union was consummated, and the present star-shaped medal adopted. The names of the Knights appeared in the catalogues as members of both clubs, and the second executive officer was rechristened "the Deputy Master," — an anomaly that was subsequently recognized, and a return to the older form authorized by vote.

It was now evident that the augmented property of the Club required better housing and protection against the risks of removals and possibly of eviction; for we were then the tenants, vicariously, of the College, and could not always count upon the benevolence of the authorities. Whatever the Club owned had been, nevertheless, well regulated, notably since 1820, when the present distribution of officers was made among the classes, and Jerome Napoleon Bonaparte, the Secretary, assisted by Hilary Breton Cenas, the Librarian, devised methods of order that are still worthy of imitation; and to the former the Club is furthermore greatly indebted for the "New Code" of 1821.

Stoughton 28 was then occupied by the Librarians, and piled high with the Club's effects; accordingly, the contributions of the Knights raised an *immensa indigestaque mola* that seemed to baffle all ingenuity of arrangement. Besides, the room was not assigned by the College to a Librarian, *ex officio;* consequently, a Brother was sometimes chosen to the office perforce, if he happened to draw the number, which every Porcellian set at the head of his list to insure its retention "in the family."

Admonished by these circumstances, and compelled to the selection of a suitable domicile, a committee was appointed, and, after mature deliberation, the "Long Room" in the Athenæum Building, standing, until within the past few months, upon this site, was rented and furnished.

The last meeting in the Librarians' room was adequately celebrated on the 22d of May, 1833; and on the 6th of June the Brethren, in joyful array, proceeded to admire the bewildering evidences of the taste and foresight displayed in the preparation of their new quarters. Step by step they have advanced to the acquisition of the land and building, and, habitually conservative, they waited throughout fifty-three years of tenancy, in whole or in part, before purchasing this property.

As we praise, this evening, the architectural appropriateness of our present home, and the skill that has combined the charm of the old with the convenience and durability of the new, we can turn to the page of the Secretary of 1833, glowing with the enthusiasm of a former auspicious occasion, and read his opinion that the ancient "Long Room" was "sufficiently genteel for the reception of the most celebrated clubs of London or Paris."

Another gratifying result of the union of the Porcellians and the Knights was the Address of the Deputy; nor does it seem advisable, in this instance, to alter either the conception or form of the original. In the earlier days, the Initiatee, upon election, was without delay presented to the company, and welcomed by every Deputy after a formula of his own premeditation; the Secretaries, in their notes, often reproducing from memory several of the felicitous sentences. These were collated by Brother Heyward in 1806, and copied more than once in the Records, but merely as suggestions to the Deputies, and to those appointed yearly to deliver a "Charge" and a poem for the instruction of the Club in the precepts of our Founder.

With the appearance of the present Address, in 1834, the poem and "Charge" were in turn discontinued. Set verse and speech seldom have place in our inclosure, which has always been kept a pasture and recreation ground of the intellect, and not an arid and strenuous arena. Moreover, we may be allowed to believe that no exposition of Porcellian doctrine can surpass the lucidity and elegance of the epitome that then came to us by inheritance.

The range of eligibility for election is with us, theoretically, very wide; although, to secure perfect cordiality, our circle cannot expand beyond the limit of our unhesitating confidence and unanimous choice.

The proposal to confine Honorary Membership to graduates of the College was rejected in 1830, and again, in 1832, all University students residing in Cambridge and under observation during a year and a half were declared to be eligible; but it was not thought permissible to sanction the election of any one whose qualifications, before graduation, were concealed from his own college generation. Latterly, even a superficial acquaintance with all undergraduates is manifestly unattainable; yet, until it is demonstrated that the utmost sincerity is less than should be offered to a chosen friend, we ought to have no misgivings and few regrets. The impulses of ingenuous youth are not infallible. We are expressly warned that for them we will be held to account; but, in this place, we may trust them beyond the worldly leaven of maturity, or the precocity that fain would imitate it.

Fifteen years ago, our ex-Grand Marshal and Trustee, Augustus Thorndike Perkins, concluded an admirable sketch of the Club[1] with an enumeration of some who have gone from our midst to achieve a fame, not confined to their nationality, in Literature, Science, Art, Theology, Law, and Statesmanship, and it is our greatest satisfaction to know that the bearer of every illustrious name became a Porcellian by virtue of our quaint axiom that so significantly commends "the Feelings of a Man" before passing to "the Powers of a Scholar."

Once in our history our principles of selection were openly assailed. Members of the Junior Class appeared, on Exhibition Day of 1824, wearing a facsimile of our insignia, which they claimed to respect, and by appealing to

[1] Printed in *The Harvard Book*.

the Public attempted to draw us into a discussion. The Club, however, ignored the provocation to exchange shouts with the Cyclops, whose aims and vision were alike defective, and won the commendation of the Honorary Members by submitting to them the Records and Memoranda treating of the incident that caused the hostile demonstration.

The Spaniard, weakened by age, sought the Fountain of Youth under southern skies, in a climate where mildness savors of decay. Our Fountain attracted us when, as yet untried, we were preparing for achievement. Its surroundings are bright with the fairness of Health; and its waters, taken at the source, fortify against enervation and despondency.

Our Founder did not pretend to solve for us the gravest or highest problems of life, but he has encouraged us to meet them unselfishly and cheerfully. If this temper accompanies us to the end, and distinguishes between success and failure; if those who have learned its value are more apt than others to prefer the best and accomplish the most, then the Club is justified of the Brethren as well as of our anonymous poet, who has sung: —

"Here 's a health to our Founder, McKean,
That man of immaculate Fame,
Whose heart was so big,
Who nourished a pig,
And gave us our time-honored name.
Here 's a health to the Merry and Wise,
To Youth that is steadfast and true,
To those who supported the Club and its cause,
And whose spirit is living in you."

ODE BY BRO. HON. JOHN O. SARGENT, '30

READ BY THE GRAND MARSHAL

I.

LIVE while we live! Our fathers heard
  The ripple at the fountain's head —
By rushing waves our hearts are stirred,
  Now that a hundred years have fled.

II.

They lived in simplest fellowship,
  Content on one crisp roast to dine;
When Porter spiced and mulled their flip,
  And Medford vaults matured their wine.

III.

They did not spare the midnight oil,
  They dug their share of Hebrew roots,
But sought to mingle sport with toil,
  Play with the flowers and pluck the fruits.

IV.

The fruits! Mark on our living list,
  Or on the scroll that Death has starr'd,
The chrysalid deipnosophist
  Turn jurist, statesman, sculptor, bard.

V.

Our Allston strove for Raphael's fame,
  Our Channing taught that God is Love;
Leaps to our lips how many a name
  Of Brothers with us — or above!

VI.

Come to the front! our patriarch band,
  Furness and Winthrop, Lowell, Holmes,
While over seas we stretch the hand
  To Story — Art's delight and Rome's.

VII.

Live all the spring-tide hours of youth,
  Live all you may in waning age,
Hold fast by Honor, Friendship, Truth,
  And tireless war with Falsehood wage.

VIII.

Work! for dear Alma Mater's sake,
  Indulge her too in every whim,
And all her Athlete courses take,
  With no base care for life or limb.

IX.

Alive to Duty! shun the bog
  Of bigot zeal and party hate,
Nor dare transgress the Decalogue
  Though Senates deem it out of date.

X.

Proud of the Nation — ever be
  Obedient to her sovereign will;
Rule as she may from sea to sea,
  HOME is the freeman's fortress still.

XI.

There Woman reigns — her facile sway
  Will now persuade and now perplex;
One lady-love the young obey,
  The old admire and love — the Sex.

XII.

Two crystal rills run side by side,
  So near — that each with each unites;
Thus blended in a social tide,
  Porcellians mingled with the Knights.

XIII.

Muse, on their Medal's dual face,
  Themes for a sermon or a song;
Dear Brothers, I entreat your grace,
  If I have read its legends wrong.

POEM BY BRO. HON. H. G. CHAPMAN, '83

HERE at the mile-post of a hundred years
We open these wide doors that swing across
The threshold of our second century.
Welcome to your new home, ye that belong
To this renowned Porcellian Brotherhood;
Here to renew by hand and voice and eye
The unseverable ties that all have wound
About their lives, who in the onward course
Of this last hundred years have met a while,
And journeyed in each other's company.

For where in all the world but here
  Should truest friendship have its birth?
Where naught of any was to fear,
  Each trusting in the other's worth.

And if, with freedom grown too free,
  Some oats were somewhat wildly sown,
Our sins were public property,
  The worst there was to know was known.

Nor was it then to meet an hour
  And part a year, for other's sake,
Old Time himself was in our power,
  And wrought the chains he cannot break.

Wrought them from golden beams of sun
  Of some long summer afternoon
That fell in reach, when it was done,
  At evening of a day in June.

Wrought them the while, of a storm-swept day,
  With our books or beer and our pipes aglow,
We watched from the fire the winds at play
  With the old year's leaves or the new year's snow.

Wrought them through many a famous night,
  Summer or winter, as chance might be,
When the old walls shook and the floors took fright
  At the sound of Porcellian revelry.

Into the strands of our life are woven
  Scraps of saying and shreds of song;
And who could have told, had it not been proven,
  So strange a fetter should be so strong.

But as we grasp each other's living hands,
What do I hear without? Who 's he that stands,
With powdered wig and breeches to the knee,
There by the door? What wonderment I see
Upon his face and in his restless eye,
That seeks to recognize this company!
What if he know us not!—do we not know him?
Look in the Catalogue—does it not show him
LL. D., Mr., Rhet. et Orat. Prof.,
Boylston and *S. H. S., G. M.?*—Enough!
Not know him yet? I see your eyes grow rounder.
Joseph McKean it is, Our Honored Founder.
Make room, make room! and give the master place!
Make room, make room! that we may see his face,
Whose fame a thousand sons have boasted,
Whose name a hundred classes toasted!
Speak! speak! And as a silence falls at last
Our ancient guest speaks to us from the past:

"Gentlemen—Brothers, if you call you so:
'T was thus we spoke a hundred years ago—
When I was ushered in, you may have seen

I was much ta'en aback, and deemed I'd been
Misled, or in some manner misdirected
To a strange house, where I was not expected;
But now, from your kind welcome, I perceive
That I was right; yet how could I believe
That such a goodly fellowship had grown
Out of the little seed that I had sown;
How in this palace see our student's nook,
This library — our shelf without a book!
How could I know, who neither knew a name
Nor yet a face, that this was still the same
Porcellian Club to-day that was begun
So modestly by us in '91!
But as I stood among you in the throng,
Ere you caught sight of me, it was not long
Before I saw that, though the change was great
In many things, this luxury and state
Instead of our bare rooms, and last, not least,
These indications of a splendid feast
For which you are preparing here instead
Of our plain fare, (although I hear it said
You still serve up the sucking pig, and greet him
With honor, though you may not care to eat him,) —
Saw, that in spite of all the innovations
That time must bring in many generations,
One thing remained, one thing that you inherit
Unchanged, undimmed, the true Porcellian spirit.
This is well done; keep it and hand it on
Unchanged, undimmed, till 1991.
And while you do, my ghostly promise hear
To visit you one night each hundredth year
Henceforth forever. So to-night I'll stay
And dine with you, nor leave till break of day;
For now I see, the while I have been striving
To reassure me, others were arriving,
And I myself shall presently renew
Some early friendship here, as well as you."

Yes, of this celebration it cannot be said
We 've remembered the quick, but forgotten the dead;
For you see the Committee has sent invitations
To the ghosts of Porcellians of all generations,
And I fancy, unless I 'm mistaken, you 'll find
That there is n't a soul of them all that 's declined.
And, Brothers, indeed it 's a splendid array
Of famous old fellows we 'll have here to-day.
One would almost imagine, at seeing them all,
That we 'd opened America's Pantheon Hall.
You know them by name, but I doubt if their faces
Are quite as familiar; and then there are traces
Of a fading or dimness, that often appears
When a man 's been a ghost for a number of years.
What if people are wont to regard with severity
Those who hand their own ancestors down to posterity!
I 'm going to present them; I 'll warrant you then
That you 'll never fight shy of good spirits again.

And first, Joseph Story, our Judge and our Jurist,
The soundest, the wisest, the ablest, the purest —
But there is n't an adjunct expressive of glory
Whose superlative has n't been fastened to Story.
One would surely have thought that the quota of praise
In available use by the men of those days
Had all been applied to this marvel of men.
Not a bit, for we find that as much more again
Was freely and fairly bestowed on another,
William Ellery Channing, his classmate and brother.

Next, Washington Allston, so modestly famous
That, if we should let him, he 'd certainly blame us
For paying him even the slightest attention.
And this, by the way, too, reminds me to mention
That even in *those* days the Club was well known
For admiring itself, and for praising its own;
And Allston, while shunning the public, was planning
To paint or to write something pleasing to Channing.

Here comes Brother Everett, Prometheus unbound,
And Erasmus with learning perfected and sound,
With the voice of the Titan to thunder at Zeus,
But the heart of the scholar to find an excuse;
Who for this University broadened his knowledge,
But gave to the State what he got for the College,
Save once, when he found a few years he could spare,
And sat down for a rest in the President's chair.

And here 's Brother Curtis — 't was not very far
From the place where he stood to the top of the bar;
And Binney, our great Pennsylvanian, who sets
His State on a par with our own Massachusetts:
Great lawyers, but here is a Brother whose pen
Has helped to create many eminent men,
For the lawyers from Maine to New Mexico are sons,
Or at least sons-in-law, of Theophilus Parsons.

Next comes Brother Prescott, whose exquisite diction
Throws a halo of truth round a kernel of fiction,
For many a hall of the beautiful palace he
Built is upheld by his columns of fallacy.
Yet *œre perennius* his books bid defiance
To the drill of research and the pickaxe of Science,
That are wielded by diggers whose methods are leading
To some very good books, that make very poor reading.

And next we have Motley, whose writings they call
The finest historical novels of all:
An old-fashioned writer, who did not pursue
The historical method; I fancy it 's true,
That most of us now, when we have any leisure,
Read Ibsen for facts, and read Motley for pleasure.

But how shall I deal with the next that appear,
With Charles Francis Adams and Sumner? — I fear —
But stay! one is with us on whom I can call,
Who shall speak for himself — nay, shall speak for them all.

Let the eulogy come from those eloquent still lips
That never could flatter — I call Wendell Phillips.

(*Ghost of Wendell Phillips loquitur.*)

"It is no eulogy that I shall seek
To press upon you; I shall only speak
A word or two that cannot come amiss,
Spoken by me, at such a time as this.
True, many of us here have gained a place
On some historian's pages, who shall trace
The record of a fight that battered down
Old ties, old friendships. 'T is sad renown
That even in part stands on the overthrow
Of one's own blood, as ours must stand. I know
There was not one of us that had not joyed
To live unknown, so could he have destroyed
The causes of his fame, to be again
Brothers. Alas! we were not brothers then.
Was I a brother of our Brother Grand
Theodore Lyman, whom I sought to brand
A 'dainty gentleman,' as I was branding
His 'gentleman of property and standing'?
I was myself Grand Marshal of the Club,
Yet I could find it in my heart to dub
'One of the family' of our Judge Curtis
'Upstart attorney' — surely that must have hurt his
Judicial pride; and then I gave some notice
To Peleg Sprague, and Harrison Gray Otis.
Nor did I, in those days, refrain from scoring
Our Brothers Perkins, Oliver, and Loring,
And Sturgis too, and Jackson, all and each,
For backing up that March the seventh speech.
Therefore this hundred years has not been passed
In perfect peace among us, but at last
Not only has the general peace been sealed,
But, happily, the wounds themselves are healed;
And once again we gather, as of yore,
Though parted fifty years, brothers once more.

What shall I say for you who took the lead,
Porcellians, generals, Fitz-Hugh Lee and Meade,
Who saw and were the utter battle edge
Of those last days, will you refuse to pledge
Your Founder's health together here to-day,
And longer stand apart among us? Nay,
Meade shall forget his Gettysburg, and Lee
Forget the spring of eighteen sixty-three;
All shall forget the very word Rebellion,
No North, no South, but all of us Porcellian!"

Again your poet speaks: These are not all
Our famous memories. We must recall
Dana, whose true renown was floating past
This generation, 'lashed to a drifting mast,'
Till Adams threw a fame-preserver to him,
And saved him 'as he was to those who knew him;'
And old Tom Appleton, whose genial wit
Has brightened up the nether world a bit;
And Richardson, who bids me say to you
That none shall feel the loss of plans he drew
For cosy libraries, spacious hall,
For William Peters has outdone them all.
All these are here to-night, and many others,
The ghosts of no less memorable Brothers,
Around our genial hearth are swarming,
To celebrate our new house-warming.

Those who are dead salute you; they are free
To vanish if they like not poetry.
Besides, they 're not in any wise to blame
For adding *this* to my poetic fame.
The rest of you will have to stay and bear it;
You made me write it, and I 'll make you hear it.

I find, I confess with much surprise,
That some of us fail to realize

What a very large part the old Club plays
In the outside world, in these latter days;
Yet, if you 'll allow me to point it out,
I think you 'll admit that beyond a doubt
Art and science and law and letters
Are all of them hopelessly our debtors.
Find me the best, and his best degree
Is a white pig's head and a green P. C.;
And in any profession the man at the head 'll
Turn out to be the one who 's explained his medal.
And first the poets. Besides myself
There 's Sargent and Wister to start the shelf,
And one or two others, whose books would show well,
If prettily bound — say Holmes and Lowell.
For he is ours who has cast a spell
That has doomed us forever, wherever we dwell,
Some by adoption and some by birth,
To carry New England round the earth —
Oliver Wendell Holmes, who wrote,
On one occasion, if I may quote,
That "Little of all we value here
Wakes on the morn of its hundredth year
Without both feeling and looking queer."
And yet this morning the Club awoke
As strong as iron, as sound as oak;
And I think an initiatee could tell
That it never has looked or felt so well.
Ah! Doctor Holmes, the 'one-hoss shay'
Ran just a hundred years to a day —
Give one more day to the Club, and then
Your moral may be applied again;
For to-morrow morning the Club, I fear,
May wake both looking and feeling queer.

And Lowell — you cannot suppose I 'd insert him
In that casual manner and promptly desert him —
A poet who wanders from gay to pathetic,
Onomatopoetical, peripatetic.

First touching our hearts as he knows how to do it, he
Next flashes out with some wild incongruity,
Making us roar at his smooth ingenuity.
O father of strange multiverbial rhymes,
Pray tell us why politics bores us at times,
When the mind, finding out what an idol it is, shuns
The goddess that 's worshiped by all politicians —
The Goddess of Fame, and their private ambitions.
Yet this is a time when we hardly can dodge
Certain questions presented by one Cabot Lodge,
Who 's fathered and asks us to swallow the Force Bill,
Like a physical fact or a page of the Gospel.
Still, those who feel sorry for him, Heaven knows have felt
Worse at the plight of poor Theodore Roosevelt,
Who at present 's in search of a lecture room where he can
Lecture without being called 'un-American;'
And Perry, whose quasi-magnhominous air
Has increased with increasing Congressional care,
Was quite gay when he left us, but now he has grown
To be sort of a Belmont committee of one.

Now of course I could keep up this qualified praise,
With the subjects I have, for a number of days,
But what I have given, I think, will be ample
As specimens, mounted by way of example,
Just one out of ten, as you frequently see 'em
In any well-organized modern museum.
To be really complete would take several poems;
Thus I 've mentioned but one of the family Holmes,
To wit, the Holmes *Medico-poeticalis;*
Though of course there 's Holmes *Sapiens judicialis* —
The first man of science (for England) to draw
The lines on which luck has evolved into law.
I wish, too, I had just a little more time an'
A little more space for the family Lyman,
Whose regular blooms are of excellent sort,
But which once blossomed out with a very rare sport,

Our Great-Great-Grand Marshal, whose sufferings we share,
And who has our best wish when we wish he were here.
But, Brothers, in spite of the marvelous showing
We make as a whole, there is really no knowing
How little each separate man might have done,
If each had engaged in the struggle alone;
What severe competition and rivalry must
Have occurred, if we never had had a Porc. Trust.
Yet we fear not the courts, nor the next Legislature;
Our charter 's drawn after the statutes of nature,
A close corporation, whose method is plain —
Get into what 's going, and being in, stay in.
Dum vivimus, while we 're about it, we say;
Vivamus, let 's do things in shape, and make hay
While the sun shines, a motto that gives us good measure,
For it puts into work what it takes out of pleasure.
And frankly, I think there are plenty of creeds
That fall shorter by far of humanity's needs.
Let 's follow it, then, both in letter and spirit,
And if we don't reach it we 'll come pretty near it,
While year after year this Porcellian fraternity
Sends the Universe booming along to Eternity.

FEBRUARY DINNER

At a little after seven o'clock the Brothers all assembled in the large Dining Room for the Annual Dinner, Grand Marshal George B. Shattuck presiding. The Literary Exercises having preceded the Dinner, speeches were not called for during the evening; but the Brothers received with enthusiastic applause speeches from Brother J. L. Carroll, '50, and from Brother W. W. Greenough, '37, who replied to the toast of the "Oldest Living Graduate Present." The following are some of the songs which were given during the evening: —

"The Oldest Living Graduate" . . .	C. F. Sprague, '79
"I never Drink behind the Bar" . .	R. P. Carroll, '85
"Show me the Scotchman"	L. H. Morgan, '89 G. B. Painter, '89 H. M. Sears, '89 P. S. Sears, '89
"The Oak and the Ash and the Bonny Ivy Tree"	R. D. Sears, '83
"Are you there, Moriarty?"	W. Y. Peters, '81
"The Dude who Did n't Dance" . .	G. B. Painter, '89
"The little Black Bull came down from the Mountain"	F. W. Bradlee, '60
The "Club Song"	F. W. Bradlee, '60

The many amusing incidents of the evening and the toasts of the officers of the Club are recorded in full in the Record Book of the Club.

DIAGRAM OF THE TA

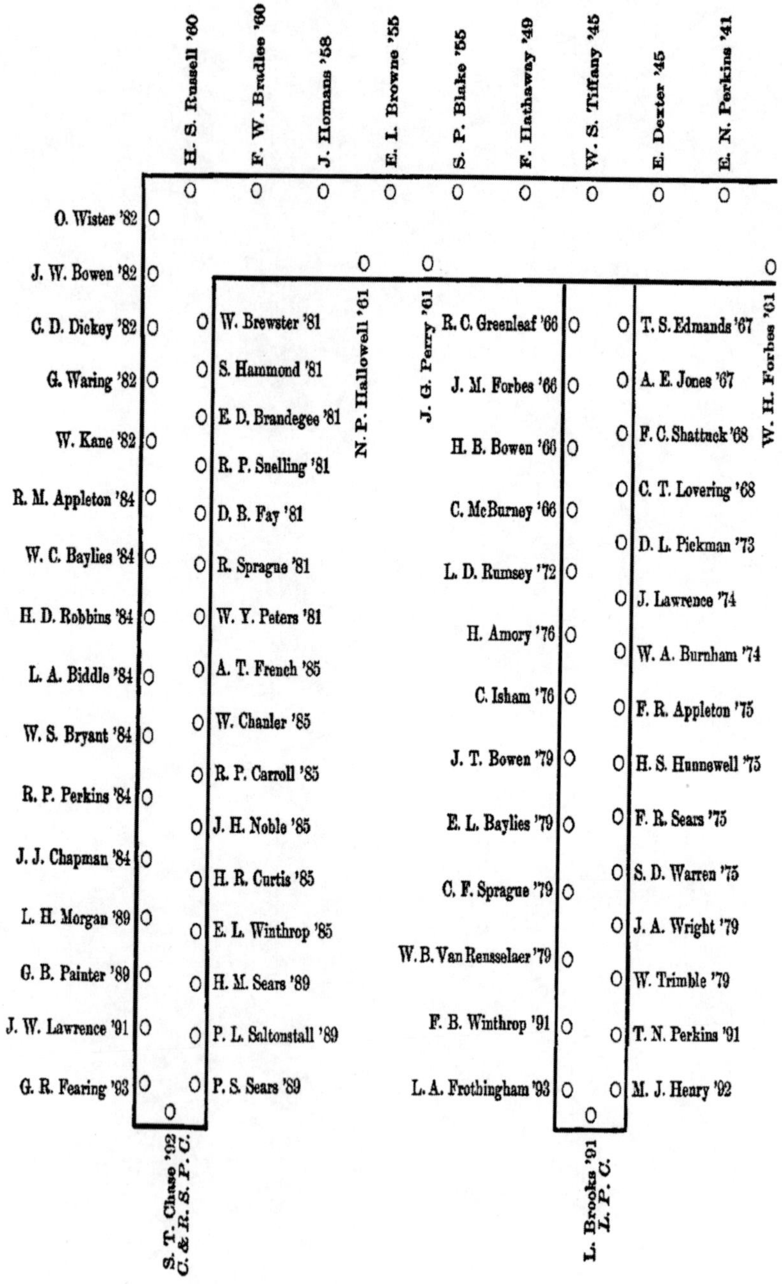

: (153 *Members present*).

W. W. Greenough '37
G. M. Lane '40
J. L. Carroll '50
H. Hathaway '50
S. L. Thorndike '52
T. Chase '53
E. W. Codman '54
B. J. Jeffries '54
S. Hammond

A. Amory '62.
H. P. Quincy '62
N. Appleton '63
J. A. Rumrill '50

R. Codman '64
R. H. Derby '64
G. H. Mifflin '65
J. R. Chadwick '65
F. I. Amory '71
J. Brown '71
W. Clifford '71
F. T. Brown '77
A. C. Tower '77
F. Peabody
P. V. R. Ely '78
E. Blaine '78
F. N. Watriss '92
W. Amory '92

N. Longworth '91
D. M'l

C. W. Amory '63
A. L. Mason '63
J. C. Warren '63
J. Winthrop '63
R. Amory '63
F. H. Appleton '69
L. M. Sargent '70
G. H. Adams '70
A. B. Denny '77
E. S. Martin '77
J. Homans '78
J. Parker '78
H. E. Teschemacher '78
F. Skinner '92
C. C. Baldwin '93

R. D. Sears '83
H. B. Cabot '83
C. P. Curtis '83
H. F. Sears '83
H. G. Chapman '83
C. Carroll '87
G. Dexter '87
E. Flagg '87
J. L. Snelling '87
F. Remington '87
G. Gray '89
G. H. Norman '89
R. I. Crocker '90
F. R. Bangs '91
R. L. Agassiz '92

I. Amory '92
Treas.

C. M. Weld '80
R. Trimble '80
R. M. Saltonstall '80
G. L. Peabody '86
D. C. Clark '86
F. S. Parker '86
O. W. Bird '86
G. L. Winthrop '86
C. Bohlen '88
J. W. Appleton '88
J. W. Wood '88
J. H. Sedgwick '88
J. S. Tooker '88
M. Agassiz '89
J. W. Smith '89
A. Amory '90
R. F. Parker '90
G. Norman '90
J. A. Burden '93

The diagram, which is given, shows how the one hundred and fifty-three Brothers present were seated. There are undoubtedly some errors in the arrangement, owing to the fact that at the last moment several Brothers were prevented from coming, while others turned up unexpectedly.

CATALOGUE

ABBREVIATIONS

G. M'l . .	Grand Marshal.
D. M'l . .	Deputy Marshal.
Tr. . . .	Trustee.
G. M. . . .	Grand Master.
D. M. . .	Deputy Master.
L. P. C. . .	Librarian P. C.
¶ . . .	Members of the P. C. and K. S. T.
* . . .	Deceased.
S. T. D. . .	Doctor of Divinity.

OLD CLUB HOUSE

PORCELLIAN CLUB, 1791

GRAND MARSHALS

*CHARLES CUTLER,	from 1792 to 1794
*JOSEPH McKEAN,	" 1794 " 1798
*CHARLES DAVIS,	" 1798 " 1800
*FRANCIS DANA CHANNING,	" 1800 " 1803
*SAMUEL PHILLIPS PRESCOTT FAY,	" 1803 " 1807
*DAVID STODDARD GREENOUGH,	" 1807 " 1811
*WILLIAM SMITH,	" 1811 " 1812
*SAMUEL DEXTER WARD,	" 1812 " 1813
*EDWARD HUTCHINSON ROBBINS,	" 1813 " 1814
*THEODORE LYMAN,	" 1814 " 1815
*MARSHALL BINNEY SPRING,	" 1815 " 1817
*MARTIN BRIMMER,	" 1817 " 1818
*EDMUND KIMBALL,	" 1818 " 1821
*WILLIAM HARVARD ELIOT,	" 1821 " 1824
*AUGUSTUS THORNDIKE,	" 1824 " 1828
*RUSSELL STURGIS,	" 1828 " 1831
*THOMAS KEMPER DAVIS,	" 1831 " 1834
*WENDELL PHILLIPS,	" 1834 " 1837
CHARLES ALFRED WELCH,	" 1837 " 1840
*SAMUEL PARKMAN,	" 1840 " 1843
*KIRK BOOTT,	" 1843 " 1846
*FRANCIS L. LEE,	" 1846 " 1848
EDWARD DEXTER,	" 1848 " 1850
*HENRY AUSTIN WHITNEY,	" 1850 " 1852
EDWARD BANGS,	" 1852 " 1856
*AUGUSTUS THORNDIKE PERKINS,	" 1856 " 1860
THEODORE LYMAN,	" 1860 " 1866
EDWARD INGERSOLL BROWNE,	" 1866 " 1869
FREDERICK WAINWRIGHT BRADLEE,	" 1869 " 1871

JOHN COLLINS WARREN,	from 1871 to 1875
*AUGUSTUS THORNDIKE PERKINS,	" 1875 " 1877
*JOSEPH SWETT COOLIDGE,	" 1877 " 1879
HENRY STURGIS RUSSELL,	" 1879 " 1881
FREDERICK CHEEVER SHATTUCK,	" 1881 " 1885
AMOS LAWRENCE MASON,	" 1885 " 1888
GEORGE BRUNE SHATTUCK,	" 1888

DEPUTY MARSHALS

*Francis Johonnot Oliver	1795
*John Heard	1795
*John Pickering	1796
*Stephen Cogswell	1797
*Samuel Phillips Prescott Fay	1798
*Abner Bartlett	1799
*John Henry Tudor	1800
*Robert Hallowell Gardiner	1801
*Leverett Saltonstall	1802
*James Savage	1803
*Leonard Kimball	1804
*Tench Tilghman	1805
*Benjamin Binney Osgood	1806
*William Coffin Harris	1807
*William Smith	1807
*Charles Cotesworth Pinckney	1808
*William Elliott	1809
*Francis Calley Gray	1809
*Theodore Lyman	1810
*Edwin Smith	1811
*Edward Hutchinson Robbins	1812
*James Rose	1813
*Julius Henry Walker	1814
*William Augustus Warner	1815
*Augustus Thorndike	1816
*Thomas Russell Sullivan	1817
*Joseph Gilman	1818
*Charles Lyman	1819
*William George Read	1820
*William Foster Otis	1821
*Larz Anderson	1822
George Peabody	1823

*Daniel Clark Relf	1824
*George Augustus Beverly Walker	1825
*Paul Trapier	1825
*Jerome Napoleon Bonaparte	1826
*Francis Dwight	1827
Robert Charles Winthrop	1828
*Edward Patrick Milliken	1829
*John Bryant	1830
*Wendell Phillips	1831
*Joseph Stevens Buckminster Thacher	1832
*Fletcher Webster	1833
*Charles Henry Wheelwright	1834
William Henry Allen	1835
*Thomas Pinckney Rutledge	1835
John Thompson Gray	1836
*Henry Hubbard	1837
*James Barnwell Heyward	1838
*George William Christy	1839
*Thomas Snead	1839
*John Francis Heath	1840
Edward Newton Perkins	1841
George Theodore Lyman	1842
*Charles Callahan Perkins	1843
*Charles William Dabney	1844
Edward Dexter	1845
*William Ellery Sedgwick	1846
*Charles Henry Morrell	1847
Joseph Pringle Alston	1848
Martin Brimmer	1849
Walter Channing Cabot	1850
*William Nye Davis	1851
Samuel Lothrop Thorndike	1852
*William Henry Cunningham	1853
Robert Charles Winthrop	1854
Theodore Lyman	1855
Francis Blake Rice	1856
*John Julius Pringle Alston	1857
Josiah Bradlee	1858
*Heyward Cutting	1859
Caspar Crowninshield	1860

Norwood Penrose Hallowell 1861
Henry Upham Jeffries 1862
Amos Lawrence Mason 1863
Richard Codman 1864
William Lawrence Tucker 1865
George Derby Welles 1866
Thomas Sprague Edmands 1867
Dawes Eliot Furness 1868
Francis Henry Appleton 1869
*Stephen Van Rensselaer Thayer 1870
James Patterson Scott 1871
Alanson Tucker 1872
Frederick Getman Fincke 1873
James Lawrence 1874
Francis Randall Appleton 1875
Samuel Sherwood 1876
*Henry Upham 1877
James Parker 1878
Otho Holland Williams 1879
Henry Russell Shaw 1880
George Phinehas Upham 1881
Woodbury Kane 1882
Charles Pelham Curtis 1883
Robert Patterson Perkins 1884
Winthrop Chanler 1885
Oliver Ames 1886
John Linzee Snelling 1887
Franklin Remington 1887
James Waldingfield Appleton 1888
Lewis Henry Morgan 1889
Richard Fay Parker 1890
Nicholas Longworth 1891

TRUSTEES

LIBRARIANS

*Joseph Sprague	1804
*Robert Smith	1805
*Daniel Oliver	1806
*John Glenn King	1807
*Henry Pierce	1808
*Francis Calley Gray	1809
*Thomas Amory Dexter	1810
*William Smith	1811
*George Washington Heard	1812
*Benjamin Huger	1813
*Martin Brimmer	1814
*Joseph Orne	1815
*Henry Artemas Ward	1816
*Oliver Sheafe	1817
*Nathaniel Hathaway	1818
*Samuel Taylor Gilman	1819
*Charles Paine	1820
*David Wood Gorham	1821
*William Yates	1822
*Russell Sturgis	1823
*Charles Gideon Putnam	1824
*Hilary Breton Cenas	1825
*Adolphus Peter Jouve	1826
*Thomas Dwight	1827
*Francis Caleb Loring	1828
*Ezra Weston	1829
*John Bozman Kerr	1830
*Robert Habersham	1831
*Samuel Parkman Shaw	1832
*William Dehon	1833
Joseph Hartwell Williams	1834
William Frederick Frick	1835

*Grenville Tudor Phillips	1836
*Christopher Columbus Holmes	1837
*John Francis Tuckerman	1837
*Benjamin Smith Rotch	1838
*Romuald Labranche	1839
*James Lawrence	1840
*Henry Fowle Durant	1841
Benjamin White Nichols	1842
Frederick Richard Sears	1843
Stephen Goodhue Wheatland	1844
Harrison Ritchie	1845
Thomas R. Rodman	1846
William Crowninshield Endicott	1847
James Steuart Thorndike	1848
*Joseph Swett Coolidge	1849
*Edmund Lincoln Baylies	1850
*Francis Oliver Dabney	1851
George Augustus Peabody	1852
Charles Coolidge Pomeroy	1853
Charles Thorndike	1854
Edward Ingersoll Browne	1855
George Bigelow Chase	1856
*Howard Dwight	1857
*Hollis Hunnewell	1858
James Augustus Rumrill	1859
John Wells Hunnewell	1860
*Thomas Rodman Robeson	1861
*Benjamin Crowninshield Mifflin	1862
Albert Chevalier Hazeltine	1863
John Alvarez Dillon	1864
George Harrison Mifflin	1865
Thomas Sargeant Perry	1866
*William Homer	1867
Augustus George Bullock	1868
Franklin Bartlett	1869
William Austin Wadsworth	1870
William Tudor	1871
*Richard Augustine Gambrill	1872
James Cleaves Dodge	1873
Charles Sanders Tuckerman	1874

MORNING ROOM—OLD CLUB

Francis Shaw	1875
Charles Isham	1876
Truman Heminway	1877
Emmons Blaine	1878
Charles Franklin Sprague	1879
Theodore Roosevelt	1880
Richard Sprague	1881
Charles Denston Dickey	1882
Henry Francis Sears	1883
Walter Cabot Baylies	1884
Amos Tuck French	1885
William Reynolds Wilson	1886
Gordon Dexter	1887
Charles Bohlen	1888
George Blair Painter	1889
Hollis Horatio Hunnewell	1890
Lawrence Brooks	1891

SECRETARIES

	Class of
*Joseph McKean	1794
*Amos Kent	1795
*John Pickering	1796
*John Russell	1796
*Horace Binney	1797
*John Joy	1797
*Samuel Phillips Prescott Fay	1798
*John William Caldwell	1799
*David Ireland Greene	1800
*John Henry Tudor	1800
*William Bant Sullivan	1801
*James Skidmore Dunning	1802
*Ray Clarke	1803
*Leonard Kimball	1804
*Tench Tilghman	1805
*James Heyward	1806
*Benjamin Binney Osgood	1806
*William Coffin Harris	1807
*Samuel M. A. Storrow	1808
*Charles Cotesworth Pinckney	1808
*William Elliott	1809
*Theodore Lyman	1810
*Edwin Smith	1811
*Edward Everett	1811
*Edward Hutchinson Robbins	1812
*James Rose	1813
*Julius Henry Walker	1814
*Martin Brimmer	1814
*William Augustus Warner	1815
*Augustus Thorndike	1816
*Thomas Russell Sullivan	1817
*Joseph Gilman	1818
*Charles Lyman	1819

	Class of
*John Haslett	1819
*William Gore Read	1820
*William Foster Otis	1821
*Daniel Wikoff	1822
George Peabody	1823
*George Augustus Beverly Walker	1825
*William Miller	1825
*Jerome Napoleon Bonaparte	1826
*Francis Dwight	1827
Robert Charles Winthrop	1828
*William Henry Channing	1829
*Edward Patrick Milliken	1829
*John Bryant	1830
*Abraham Rand Thompson	1831
*Robert Habersham	1831
*Richard Miller Chapman	1832
*Francis Eben Oliver	1833
*Gervais Baillio	1833
Joseph Hartwell Williams	1834
William Henry Allen	1835
William Minot	1836
Samuel Gray Ward	1836
*Henry Hubbard	1837
*Benjamin Smith Rotch	1838
*Romuald Labranche	1839
*James Lawrence	1840
Edward Newton Perkins	1841
*Charles Callahan Perkins	1843
James Gordon Clarke	1844
Edward Dexter	1845
*Henry Austin Whitney	1846
William Crowninshield Endicott	1847
*Colin Mackenzie	1847
Joseph Pringle Alston	1848
Francis Hathaway	1849
Abbott Lawrence	1849
*Augustus Thorndike Perkins	1851
Samuel Lothrop Thorndike	1852
*William Henry Cunningham	1853

	Class of
Theodore Chase	1853
Robert Charles Winthrop	1854
*Payson Perrin Ellis	1855
*Charles Le Doux Elgee	1856
Francis Blake Rice	1856
*John Julius Pringle Alston	1857
Benjamin William Crowninshield	1858
*Heyward Cutting	1859
Caspar Crowninshield	1860
James Henry Wilson	1860
*Francis Lowell Gardner	1862
*Herbert Cowpland Mason	1862
Amos Lawrence Mason	1863
James Lewis Pearce	1863
John Collins Warren	1863
Richard Codman	1864
William Lawrence Tucker	1865
Charles Heber McBurney	1866
Dawes Eliot Furness	1868
Francis Henry Appleton	1869
Dudley Pickman Rogers	1869
Lucius Manlius Sargent	1870
James Patterson Scott	1871
Charles Howland Russell	1872
Perry Belmont	1872
Dudley Leavitt Pickman	1873
Francis Randall Appleton	1875
Samuel Sherwood	1876
George Barnwell Ogden	1877
James Parker	1878
Charles Franklin Sprague	1879
Henry Russell Shaw	1880
George Phinehas Upham	1881
James William Bowen	1882
Henry Grafton Chapman	1883
Richard Dudley Sears	1883
Walter Cabot Baylies	1884
Royal Phelps Carroll	1885
Francis Stanley Parker	1886

	Class of
Oliver Ames	1886
John Linzee Snelling	1887
Copley Amory	1888
George Blair Painter	1889
William Astor Chanler	1890
Richard Fay Parker	1890
John Watson Lawrence	1891
Samuel Thompson Chase	1892

KNIGHTS OF THE SQUARE TABLE, 1809

GRAND MASTERS

ACC.		EX.
1810	*JOHN APPLETON HAVEN	1813
1813	*JAMES WALKER	1814
1814	*JOHN GORHAM PALFREY	1815
1815	*SAMUEL PERRY	1816
1816	*FRANCIS WILLIAM WINTHROP	1817
1817	*WINSLOW WARREN SEAVER	1818
1818	*THOMAS SAVAGE CLAY	1819
1819	*JOSEPH THORNTON ADAMS	1820
1820	*WILLIAM FOSTER OTIS	1821
1821	*NORMAN SEVER	1822
1822	GEORGE PEABODY	1823
1823	*GEORGE AUGUSTUS BEVERLY WALKER	1824
1824	*WILLIAM HAZARD WIGG BARNWELL	1825
1825	*FRANCIS CUNNINGHAM	1826
1826	*BENJAMIN VARNUM CROWNINSHIELD	1827
1827	*FRANCIS DWIGHT	1828
1828	BENJAMIN DUICK WHITNEY	1829
1829	EDWARD LINZEE CUNNINGHAM	1830
1830	JOHN OSBORNE SARGENT	1831
1831	*HENRY FREDERICK FRIESE	1831

DEPUTY MASTERS

ACC.		EX.
1810	* William Jones Spooner	1811
1811	* Pliny Merrick	1812
1812	* John Gorham Palfrey	1813
1813	* Samuel Perry	1814
1814	* Francis William Winthrop	1815
1815	* Grenville Mellen	1816
1816	* Henry Upham	1817
1817	* Alfred Woodward Haven	1818
1818	* Samuel Hall Lyon	1819
1819	* Norman Seaver	1820
1820	George Peabody	1821
1821	* George Augustus Beverly Walker	1822
1822	* William Miller	1824
1824	* Benjamin Varnum Crowninshield	1825
1825	Robert Charles Winthrop	1826
1826	* Ezra Weston	1827
1827	* John James Gilchrist	1828
1828	* Isaac Edward Morse	1829
1829	* Joseph Lyman	1830
1830	* Samuel Wigglesworth	1831

SECRETARIES

	Class of
*Stevens Everett	1815
*William Ware	1816
*William Bowen Oliver Peabody	1816
*Thomas Russell Sullivan	1817
*Samuel Atkins Eliot	1817
*Grenville Mellen	1818
*Stephen Clarendon Phillips	1819
*Thomas Bulfinch Coolidge	1819
*Charles Paine	1820
*Samuel Hall Lyman	1821
*Francis Dwight	1827
*George Chapman	1828
*Francis Caleb Loring	1828
*Solomon Martin Jenkins	1829
John Osborne Sargent	1830
*Charles Henry Tilghman	1831
*Alanson Tucker	1832

MORNING ROOM—NEW CLUB

PORCELLIAN CLUB

1891

GRAND MARSHAL.

GEORGE BRUNE SHATTUCK.

DEPUTY MARSHAL.

NICHOLAS LONGWORTH.

LIBRARIAN.

LAWRENCE BROOKS.

SECRETARY.

SAMUEL THOMPSON CHASE.

TREASURER.

INGERSOLL AMORY.

MEMBERS OF P. C. TO 1811

Names in capitals, Governors, Congressmen, and Judges ; those in italics, Clergymen. All towns without state name are in Massachusetts. Members' places of residence are those they had while in college.

1792

*Henderson Inches, *A. M.*	Boston.
*Robert Treat Paine, *A. M.*	Boston.

1793

*JOHN CURTIS CHAMBERLAIN, *A. M.;* Hon. Dart. 1805, *M. C.*	Worcester.
*Charles Cutler, *A. M.; G. M'l,*	Boston.
*FRANCIS GARDNER, *A. M.; M. C.*	Worcester.
*CHARLES JACKSON, *A. M.;* Overseer; *LL. D.* 1821. Just. Supr. Court, Mass.	Newburyport.
*William Jones, *A. M.*	Concord.
*Francis Cabot Lowell, *Hon. Mem.* 1793; *A. M.*	Roxbury.

1794

*George Washington Appleton, *A. M.*	Boston.
*CHARLES HUMPHREY ATHERTON, *A. M.; M. C.*	Amherst, N. H.
*John Atkinson, *A. M.*	New York, N. Y.
*William Biglow, *A. M.* 1804,	Cambridge.
*Luke Brown,	Worcester.
*Francis Dana Channing, *A. M.; G. M'l,*	Newport, R. I.
*Thomas Geyer, *A. M.*	Boston.
**Joseph McKean, A. M.; LL. D.* Coll. N. J. 1814; *S. T. D.* Allegheny 1817; Boylston Prof. Rhet. and Orat.; Memb. Mass. Hist. Soc.	Boston.

*Israel Eliot Trask, *A. M.* Vermont.
*Hall Tufts, *A. M.* Medford.

1795

*Seth Bemis, *A. M.* Watertown.
*Benjamin Gorham, *A. M.; M. C.* Charlestown.
*John Heard, *A. M.; D. M'l,* Boston.
*John Whitefield Hulbert, 1805, *A. M.* 1805; *M. C.* ———
*Ebenezer Hunt, *A. M.* Northampton.
*Amos Kent, *A. M.* Newburyport.
*John Kittredge, Andover.
*Francis Johonnot Oliver, *A. M.; A. M.* Yale 1799; *D. M'l,* Boston.
*John Phillips, *A. M.* Andover.
*Josiah Sturges, *A. M.* 1800, New York, N. Y.
*Joshua Upham, St. John, N. B.

1796

*Charles George Cabot, *A. M.* 1805, Brookline.
*Charles Cushing, *A. M.* Hingham.
*Francis Dana, *A. M.* Cambridge.
*Charles Davis, *A. M.; G. M'l,* Boston.
*James Jackson, *A. M.; M. B.* 1802; *M. D.* 1809; *LL. D.* 1854; Hersey Prof. Theor. and Pract. Phys., and Prof. Emeritus; Overseer; Pres. Am. Acad.; Memb. Am. Philos. Soc.; Hon. Memb. Roy. Med. Chirurg. Soc. London, Boston.
*John Pickering, *A. M.; LL. D.* 1835, Bowd. 1822; Overseer; Pres. Am. Acad.; Memb. Mass. Hist. Soc., and Am. Philos. Soc. Boston.
*John Russell, ———
*Peter Oxenbridge Thacher, *A. M.;* Fellow Am. Acad. Boston.
*Edmund Toppan, *A. M.* Hampton, N. H.
*William Tudor, *A. M.* Boston.
*Samuel Welles, *A. M.* Boston.
*George Wingate, *A. M.* Stratham, N. H.

1797

*Horace Binney, *A. B.* (Hon.) Brown 1797; *A. M.; LL. D.* 1827; Memb. Am. Philos. Soc.; Hon. Memb. Mass. Hist. Soc.; Fellow Am. Acad.; *M. C.* Watertown.
*William Blanchard, *A. M.* Wilmington.
*Thaddeus Brown, *A. M.* Tewksbury.
*Thomas Cary, *A. M.* ———
*Stephen Cogswell, *A. M.; D. M'l,* Littleton.
*Thomas Fargues, *M. D.* 1831; also Edinburgh, Quebec, L. C.
*John Joy, Boston.
*William Ladd, Portsmouth, N. H.
*Robert Turnbull, Petersburg, Va.
*William Wetmore, *A. M.* Boston.
*John Shirley Williams, *A. M.* Boston.

1798

*Isaac Adams, *A. M.* Newbury.
*William Austin, *A. M.* Charlestown.
**William Ellery Channing*, *A. M.* 1802; *S. T. D.* 1820; Fellow; Dexter Lect.; Fellow Am. Acad. Boston.
*Isaiah Cushing, *A. M.* Hingham.
*Samuel Phillips Prescott Fay, *A. M.; D. M'l,* also *G. M'l,* Cambridge.
*Isaac Fiske, *A. M.* Weston.
*Rudolph Hill French, *A. M.* Salem.
*John Hamilton, *A. M.* 1802, Berwick.
*Moses Hook, Salisbury.
*Thomas Lee, 1866, Beverly.
*Stephen Longfellow, *LL. D.* Bowd. 1828; *M. C.* Portland, Me.
*Nathaniel Lord, *A. M.* Ipswich.
*Artemas Sawyer, Lancaster.
*George Sheafe, Portsmouth, N. H.
*Joseph Story, *A. M.; LL. D.* 1821, Brown 1815, Dart. 1824; Dane Prof. Law; Overseer; Fellow; Fellow Am. Acad.; Memb. Mass. Hist. Soc., Am. Philos. Soc.; Just. Supr. Court U. S.; *M. C.* Cambridge.

*Richard Sullivan, *A. M.;* Fellow Am. Acad.	Boston.
*Ebenezer Thatcher, *A. M.*	Cambridge.
*Gideon Latimer Thayer, *A. M.*	Braintree.
*Arthur M. Walter,	Boston.
*Thomas Welsh, *A. M.*	Boston.

1799

*Abner Bartlett, *A. M.; D. M'l,*	Plymouth.
*John William Caldwell, *A. M.*	Worcester.
*Freeman Foster,	Scituate.
*Elnathan Haskell,	Rochester.
*Timothy Pickering, *A. M.*	Lucerne Co., Pa.
*Luther Richardson, *Hon. Mem.* 1800, *A. M.*	Boston.
*Samuel John Sprague, *A. M.*	Lancaster.
*Joseph Williston,	———
*Rufus Wyman, *A. M.* 1804; *M. B.* 1804; *M. D.* 1811; Fellow Am. Acad.	Charlestown.

1800

*Washington Allston, Fellow Am. Acad.	Cambridge.
*Loammi Baldwin, *Hon. Mem.* 1806; *A. M.;* Fellow Am. Acad.	Charlestown.
*Henry Cabot, *Hon. Mem.* 1802,	Boston.
*Samuel Deane Freeman, *Hon. Mem., A. M.*	Portland, Me.
*David Ireland Greene, *A. M.*	Boston.
*Rufus Hosmer, *A. M.*	Concord.
*LEONARD JARVIS, *A. M.; M. C.*	Cambridge.
*John Knapp, *A. M.*	Boston.
*Isaac Lincoln, *A. M.; A. M.* (Hon.) Bowd. 1806; *M. D.* (Hon.) Bowd. 1831,	Hingham.
**Charles Lowell, A. M.; S. T. D.* 1823; Fellow; Memb. Mass. Hist. Soc., Kon. Norsk. Vidensk. Selsk.; Cor. Memb. Soc. Archéol. d'Athènes,	Roxbury.
*Israel Munroe, *A. M.*	Northborough.
*John Prince,	Salem.
*Aaron Hall Putnam, *A. M.*	Charlestown.
*John Henry Tudor, *A. M.; D. M'l,*	Boston.
*Ebenezer Tucker Warren, *A. M.*	Boston.
*Benjamin Welles,	Boston.

1801

*Samuel Mather Crocker, Boston.
*John Forrester, *A. M.* Salem.
*Robert Hallowell Gardiner, *A. M.; D. M'l,* Gardiner, Me.
*John Gorham, *A. M.; M. B.* 1804; *M. D.* 1811; Adjunct Prof. Chem.; Erving Prof. Chem.; Fellow Am. Acad. Boston.
*Moody Kent, *A. M.* Chichester, N. H.
**George O'Kill Stuart, A. M.* 1815; *S. T. D.* 1848; *LL. D.* King's Coll. (Windsor, N. S.) 1832; Archdeacon Kingston (Canada); Dean Ontario, Kingston, U. C.
*William Bant Sullivan, *A. M.* Boston.
*George Sullivan, *A. M.* Boston.
*William Starkey Titcomb, *A. M.* Newburyport.

1802

*Henry Babcock, *A. M.* Boston.
*John Ball, Charleston, S. C.
*John Ambourloin Brimmer, *A. M.;* also Yale 1805, Roxbury.
*William A. Bond, Boston.
*Alexander S. Brooks, Medford.
*Joseph Blake Caldwell, *A. M.* 1806, Worcester.
**John Codman, A. B.* (Hon.) Yale 1802; *A. M.; A. M.* (Hon.) Brown 1814; *S. T. D.* 1840, Coll. N. J., 1822; Memb. Mass. Hist. Soc. Boston.
*James Skidmore Dunning, New York, N. Y.
*James Henderson Elliot, *Hon. Mem.* 1803, *A. M.;* also Bowd. 1806, Boston.
*Nathaniel Fales, Boston.
*Richard Devens Harris, *A. M.* Boston.
*John King, *A. M.* Abington.
*William Minot, *A. M.* Boston.
*THOMAS ROTHMAHLER MITCHELL, *A. M.; M. C.* Georgetown, D. C.
*Timothy Newell, Sturbridge.
*Thomas Paine, *Hon. Mem.* ———
*Richard Kidder Randolph, *A. M.; LL. D.* 1840, Virginia.

*Leverett Saltonstall, *A. B.* (Hon.) Yale 1802; *A. M.; A. M.* (Hon.) Bowd. 1806; *LL. D.* 1838; Overseer; Fellow Am. Acad.; Memb. Mass. Hist. Soc.; *M. C.; D. M'l,* Salem.

1803

*George Watson Brimmer, 1806, Boston.
*Ray Clarke, Newport, R. I.
*Henry Fales, *A. M.* Boston.
*John Farrar, *A. M.; LL. D.* Brown 1833; Tutor; Hollis Prof. Math. and Nat. Philos.; Vice-Pres. Am. Acad. Cambridge.
*Simon Forrester, Salem.
*Samuel Kirkland, Boston.
*Robert Nicholson, Richmond, Va.
*Caleb Rice, *A. M.* Hingham.
*Winthrop Sargent, Boston.
*James Savage, *A. M.; LL. D.* 1841; Overseer; Fellow Am. Acad.; Pres. Mass. Hist. Soc.; *D. M'l,* Boston.
*William Bartlett Sewall, *A. M.* York, Me.
*John Man Taylor, *A. M.* Georgetown, S. C.

1804

*Thomas Aspinwall, *A. M.;* Cor. Memb. and Memb. Mass. Hist. Soc.; Memb. Kon. Norsk. Vidensk. Selsk. Boston.
*Cornelius Calvert, Norfolk, Va.
*Nathaniel Morton Davis, *A. M.* Plymouth.
*Abraham Eustis, also Bowd. 1806, *A. M.* Boston.
*Benjamin Guild, *A. M.* Boston.
*Leonard Kimball, *A. M.; D. M'l,* Boston.
*John Law, Washington, D. C.
*William Scollay, *A. M.* Boston.
*Joseph E. Sprague, *A. M.; L. P. C.* Salem.
*Samuel Cooper Thacher, *A. M.;* Librarian; Fellow; Fellow Am. Acad. Boston.
*Moses Titcomb, Portland, Me.
*Samuel Russell Trevett, *A. M.; M. B.* 1807; *M. D.* 1811. Wenham.

1805

**John Lovejoy Abbot*, *A. M.;* Librarian, Andover.
*Ebenezer Hunt Beckford, also Bowd. 1806, *A. M.* Salem.
*John Brooks, *A. M.* Medford.
*WARD CHIPMAN, *A. M.; LL. D.* 1836; Just. and Ch. Just. Sup. Court Prov. N. B. St. John, N. B.
*David Stoddard Greenough, also Yale 1805, *A. M.; G. M'l,* Roxbury.
**Hosea Hildreth*, *A. M.* Dart. 1817, Sterling.
*Abraham Fuller Hull, Newton.
*Charles Shaw, *A. M.* Bath, Me.
*Robert Smith, also Yale 1805; *L. P. C.* Charleston, S. C.
*Tench Tilghman, *D. M'l,* Talbot Co., Md.

1806

*Francis Babcock, Boston.
*Jacob Bigelow, *A. M.; M. D.* Univ. Pa. 1810; *LL. D.* 1857; Rumford Prof. and Lect. on the Application of Science to the Useful Arts; Prof. Mat. Med.; Overseer; Vice-Pres. and Pres. Am. Acad.; Memb. Am. Philos. Soc., Mass. Hist. Soc., Linnean Soc. London, Boston.
*Joseph Green Cogswell, 1807; *A. B.* (Hon.) Yale 1807; *A. M.* 1814; *Ph. D.* Göttingen 1819; *LL. D.* 1863, Trinity (Conn.) 1842; Tutor; Librarian; Prof. Mineral. and Geol.; Fellow Am. Acad.; Memb. Acad. Lit. Reg. Monacensis, Ipswich.
*Alexander Hill Everett, *A. B.* (Hon.) Yale 1807; *A. M.; LL. D.* Univ. Vt. 1826, Middlebury (Vt.) 1839; Pres. Jefferson Coll. (La.); Memb. Am. Philos. Soc.; Fellow Am. Acad.; Memb. Mass. Hist. Soc.; U. S. Min. Plen. Spain, Boston.
*William Gordon, Charlestown, N. H.
*James Heyward, Charleston, S. C.
**Isaac Hurd*, *A. M.; S. T. D.* Dart. 1854, Exeter, N. H.
*Thomas Morton Jones, also Bowd. 1806, *A. M.* Boston.

FRONT ROOM—OLD CLUB

*Benjamin Lincoln, *A. M.; M. D.* Univ. Penn. 1812, Hingham.
*George Williams Lyman, *A. M.* Boston.
*Abraham Moore, *Hon. Mem.* 1806, *A. M.* Groton.
*Daniel Oliver, *A. M.; A. M.* (Hon.) Dart. 1821; *M. D.* Univ. Pa. 1810; *LL. D.* Hobart 1838; Lect. Theor. and Pract. Med. Bowd. Coll.; Prof. Theor. and Pract. Med., Prof. Mat. Med. and Therap., Prof. Intel. Philos. Dart. Coll.; *L. P. C.* Salem.
*Benjamin Binney Osgood, *A. M.; D. M'l,* Salem.

1807

*George Bethune English, *A. M.* 1811, Cambridge.
*John Gallison, *A. M.* 1818, Marblehead.
*William Coffin Harris, *A. M.* 1838; *D. M'l,* Portsmouth, N. H.
*Nathaniel Appleton Haven, *A. M.* Portsmouth, N. H.
*John Glen King, *A. M.* 1818; *L. P. C.* Salem.
*James Otis Lincoln, *A. M.* Hingham.
*William W. Russell, Richmond, Va.
*Arthur Savage, Boston.
*David Sears, *A. M.;* Overseer, Boston.
*William Smith, *A. M.; D. M'l,* also *G. M'l,* Boston.
*William Thomas, *A. M.* Plymouth.
*Nathaniel West, *A. M.* Salem.

1808

*Edward Fenwick Campbell, *A. M.* 1812, Savannah, Geo.
*Edward Tyrrel Channing, *A. M.;* Boylston Prof. Rhet. and Orat.; *LL. D.* 1847, Cambridge.
*Walter Channing, 1867; *M. D.* (Hon.) 1812, Univ. Pa. 1809; Prof. Obstetr. and Med. Jurispr.; Dean Med. S.; Fellow Am. Acad. Boston.
*Henry Codman, *A. M.* Boston
*Isaac Foster Coffin, *Hon. Mem.* Bowd. Coll. 1806, *A. M.* Portland, Me.
*Richard Henry Dana, 1866, *LL. D.* Williams 1867, Cambridge.
*John H. Henshaw, *Hon. Mem.* 1810, Boston.

*Robert Means, *Hon. Mem.* Bowd. Coll. 1807, *A. M.* — Amherst, N. H.
*John Park, *Hon. Mem.* — Boston.
*Henry Peirce, *A. M.; L. P. C.* — Salem.
*CHARLES COTESWORTH PINCKNEY, Lt. Gov., *S. C.; D. M'l,* — Charleston, S. C.
*Hugh Rutledge, — Charleston, S. C.
*John Hannibal Sheppard, 1867; *A. M.* 1871; also Bowd. 1820, — Hallowell, Me.
*SAMUEL EMERSON SMITH, also Bowd. 1808, Gov. Maine, — Wiscasset, Me.
*Samuel M. A. Storrow, — Boston.
*George Thorndike, *Hon. Mem.* Bowd. Coll. 1806, *A. M.* — Boston.
*John Torrey, *A. M.* — Plymouth.
*David West, — Boston.

1809

*Horatio Biglow, *Hon. Mem.* 1810, *A. M.* — Cambridge.
*Kirk Boott, — Lowell.
*William Burley, — Beverly.
*Theodore Eames, *Hon. Mem.* — Haverhill.
*William Elliott, 1810; *A. M.* 1815; *D. M'l,* — Beaufort, S. C.
*Francis Calley Gray, *A. M.; LL. D.* 1841; Fellow; Memb. Mass. Hist. Soc.; Fellow Am. Acad.; *L. P. C., D. M'l,* — Boston.
*Daniel Greenleaf Ingraham, *A. M.* — Boston.
*John Lee, *A. M.* — Castine, Me.
*Nathaniel Kemble Greenwood Oliver, *A. M.* — Boston.
* *William Putnam Page, A. M.* 1814, — Danvers.
*James Perkins, — Boston.
*William Parsons Sigourney, *A. M.* — Boston.
*Samuel Dexter Ward, *G. M'l,* — Boston.

1810

*Francis Boott, *A. M.* 1814; *M. D.* Edinb.; Fellow Linnean Soc. London, and Am. Acad. — Boston.
*John Watson Davis, *A. M.* — Boston.

*Israel W. Davis,	Beverly.
*Thomas Amory Dexter, *A. M.; L. P. C.*	Boston.
*George Gay, *A. M.*	Dedham.
*Isaac Redington Howe, *A. M.*	Haverhill.
*JOSEPH GOWING KENDALL, *A. M.;* Tutor; *M. C.*	Leominster.
*Frederick Kinloch,	Georgetown, S. C.
*Theodore Lyman, *A. M.; D. M'l,* also *G. M'l,*	Boston.
*George Washington May, *A. M.* 1813,	Boston.
*John Scollay,	Boston.
*Thomas Stephens, *A. M.*	Beverly.
*Edward Strong,	Northampton.
*Henry James Tudor, *A. M*	Boston.

1811

*Charles Pelham Curtis, *Hon. Mem.* 1814, *A. M.*	Boston.
*EDWARD EVERETT, *A. M.; Ph. D.* Göttingen 1817; *LL. D.* 1835, Yale 1833, Dubl. 1842, Cambr. 1842, Dart. 1849; *J. C. D.* Oxford 1843; Tutor; Eliot Prof. Greek Lit.; Overseer; President; Memb. Am. Philos. Soc., and Mass. Hist. Soc.; Vice-Pres. Am. Acad.; Cor. Memb. Soc. Archéol. d'Athènes, and Acad. Sci. Mor. and Polit. (Institut de France); Hon. Memb. Roy. Agric. Soc. Engl., Roy. Geogr. Soc. (London), Soc. Antiq. (London), Inst. Hist. and Geogr. Brasil; Gov. Mass.; *M. C.;* Senator, Sec. State U. S.; U. S. Min. Plen. Great Britain,	Boston.
*John Chipman Gray, *A. M.; LL. D.* 1856; Overseer; Memb. Mass. Hist. Soc.; Fellow Am. Acad.	Boston.
*Robert Hooper, *A. M.*	Marblehead.
*William Powell Mason, *A. M.*	Boston.
*George Morey, *A. M.*	Walpole.
*Robert Hawkins Osgood,	Salem.
*Harrison Gray Otis, *Hon. Memb.* 1814, *A. M.*	Boston.
*Thomas Perkins, *A. M.*	Boston.
*Edward Reynolds, *A. M.; M. D.* (Hon.) Brown 1825, Bowd. 1825; Fellow Am. Acad.	Boston.
*James Russell,	Charlestown.

*John Rutledge, Charleston, S. C.
*Edwin Smith, *A. M.; D. M'l,* Wiscasset, Me.
*William Smith, *L. P. C.* St. Croix, W. I.

1812

*Isaiah Thomas Andrews, Boston.
*George Downes, Boston.
**Allston Gibbes, A. M.;* Tutor, Charleston, S. C.
*Benjamin Daniel Greene, Fellow Am. Acad. Boston.
*George Washington Heard, *A. M.; M. D.* 1815; *L. P. C.* Ipswich.
*John Homans, *A. M.; M. D.* 1815, Boston.
*George Homer, Boston.
*Edward Hutchinson Robbins, *A. M.; M. D.* 1815; *D. M'l,* also *G. M'l,* Milton.
*PELEG SPRAGUE, *A. M.; LL. D.* 1847; Judge U. S. Dist. Court (Mass.); *M. C.;* Senator U. S. Boston.
*Marshal Binney Spring, *A. M.; G. M'l,* Watertown.
*Jonathan Mayhew Wainwright, *A. M.; S. T. D.* 1835, Union 1823; *J. C. D.* Oxford 1852; Instr. Rhet. and Orat; Bishop N. Y. Boston.

At this time the order of the K. S. T. was founded. To prevent the unnecessary repetition of names, those gentlemen who were members of both Clubs are marked ¶ in the P. C. Catalogue, and those of the same Class members of the order of K. S. T. only are subjoined separately.

MEMBERS OF THE P. C. AND K. S. T. TO 1831

1813

*John Worthington Ames, — Dedham.
*John Brazer, *A. M.; S. T. D.* 1836; Tutor; Coll. Prof. Latin; Overseer; Fellow Am. Acad. — Salem.
*William Fitzhugh Carter, — Virginia.
*John Foster, — Salem.
*Washington Gibbes, — Charleston, S. C.
*Orville Luther Holley, — Salisbury, Ct.
*Benjamin Huger, *M. D.* Univ. Penn. 1817; *L. P. C.* — Charleston, S. C.
*Robert Pringle, — Charleston, S. C.
*James Rose, *A. M.; D. M'l,* — Charleston, S. C.
*John Schuyler, — Rhinebeck, N. Y.
*Theodore Sedgwick, *Hon. Mem.* — New York, N. Y.
*¶William Jones Spooner, *A. M.; D. M.* — Boston.
*¶Winslow Warren, *A. M.* 1817; *M. D.* Univ. Penn. 1817, — Plymouth.

K. S. T.

1813

*Zabdiel Boylston Adams, *A. M.; M. D.* 1816, — Roxbury.
*Gorham Bartlett, *A. M.; M. D.* 1816, — Charlestown.
*Thomas Marshall Baxter, *A. M.* — Boston.
*Charles Augustus Cheever, *A. M.; M. D.* 1816, — Lynn.
*John Appleton Haven, *A. M.; G. M.* — Portsmouth, N. H.
*Martyn Paine, *A. M.; M. D.* 1816; *LL. D.* Univ. Vt. 1854; Prof. Instit. Med. and Mat. Med., and Prof. Emeritus, Univ. City N. Y.; Cor. Memb. Kön. Ver. Heilkunde in Preussen;

Memb. Svensk. Läkare Sällsk., and Kon. Vetensk. Soc. Upsala; For. Memb. Med. Selsk. (Christiania), Williamstown, Vt.
*Daniel Parkman, *A. M.* Boston.
*GORHAM PARKS, *A. M.; M. C.* Andover.
*Henry Thompson, Charlestown.
*William Thorndike, *A. M.* Beverly.
*John Ware, *A. M.; M. D.* 1816; Hersey Prof. Theor. and Pract. Phys.; Fellow Am. Acad. Boston.
*Henry Warren, *A. M.* Boston.
*William Willis, *A. M.; LL. D.* Bowd. 1867, Portland, Me.

1814

*¶*Andrew Bigelow*, *A. M.; S. T. D.* 1844, Medford.
*Martin Brimmer, *A. M.; L. P. C.*, also *G. M'l*, Boston.
*William Cummens, 1818, Roxbury.
*George Derby, Salem.
*¶Charles Keating, Boston.
*Edmund Kimball, *G. M'l*, Newburyport.
*James G. Martin, Nashville, Tenn.
*¶Arthur Middleton, *A. M.* Charleston, S. C.
*Jonathan Porter, *A. M.* Medford.
*William Hickling Prescott, *A. M.; LL. D.* 1843, Columbia 1840, William and Mary 1841, Coll. S. C. 1841; *J. C. D.* Oxford 1850; Memb. Mass. Hist. Soc., Am. Philos. Soc.; Fellow Am. Acad.; Cor. Memb. Real Acad. Hist. (Madrid), Kön. Akad. Wissensch. (Berlin), Roy. Irish Acad. (Dublin), Soc. Geogr. y Estad. Mexico, Acad. Sci. Mor. et Polit. (Institut de France); Hon. Memb. Soc. Antiq. London, Roy. Soc. Lit. London, Boston.
*Francis Dallas Quash, *A. M.* Charleston, S. C.
*Elbridge B. Robertson, Nashville, Tenn.
*Julius Henry Walker, *A. M.* 1818; *D. M'l*, Wilmington, N. C.
*¶David Wood, Newburyport.

K. S. T

1814

*Gorham Brooks, *A. M.* Boston.
*Ephraim May Cunningham, *A. M.* Fitchburg.
*John Wendell Mellen, *A. M.* Cambridge.
*PLINY MERRICK, *A. M.; LL. D.* 1853; Overseer; Just. Supr. Court Mass. Worcester.
**James Walker, A. M.;* Div. S. 1817; *S. T. D.* 1835; *LL. D.* 1860, Yale 1853; Alford Prof. Nat. Rel., Mor. Philos. and Civ. Pol.; Fellow; Overseer; Acting President; President; Fellow Am. Acad.; Memb. Mass. Hist. Soc. Cambridge.

1815

*Thomas Aston Coffin, Charleston, S. C.
*William Harvard Eliot, *A. M.; G. M'l,* Boston.
*Arthur Mosely Henderson, Nashville, Tenn.
*William Francis Heriot, Georgetown, S. C.
*William Hooper, *A. M.* Marblehead.
*Jonathan Mason, Boston.
*¶Joseph Orne, *A. M.; L. P. C.* Salem.
**John Gorham Palfrey, A. M.;* Div. S. 1818; *S. T. D.* 1834; *LL. D.* 1869, St. Andr. 1838; Overseer; Prof. Bibl. Lit.; Memb. Mass. Hist. Soc.; *M. C.* Cambridge.
*Theophilus Parsons, *A. M.; LL. D.* 1849; Dane Prof. Law; Fellow Am. Acad.; Memb. Mass. Hist. Soc. Boston.
*Hasket Derby Pickman, Salem.
*Chandler Robbins, *Hon. Mem.* Bowd. 1815; *M. D.* 1818, Hallowell, Me.
*Benjamin Ogle Tayloe, *A. M.* 1820, Richmond, Va.
*William Augustus Warner, *A. M.; D. M'l,* Hardwick.

K. S. T.

1815

*John Prescott Bigelow, *A. M.;* also Dart. 1848, Boston.
*Daniel Neil Bradford, *A. M.; A. M.* (Hon.) Transylvania (Ky.) 1821; Tutor Transylvania Univ. Boston.
*Charles Briggs, *A. B.* (Hon.) Bowd. 1817; *A. M.;* Div. S. 1818; Tutor Bowd. Coll. Halifax, N. S.
*George Washington Eggleston, *A. M.* 1819, Lenox.
*George Eustis, *A. M.; LL. D.* 1849; Just. and Ch. Just. Supr. Court La. Boston.
**Stevens Everett*, *A. M.* Dorchester.
*Appleton Howe, *A. M.; M. D.* 1819, Hopkinton.
**George Goldthwait Ingersoll*, *A. M.; S. T. D.* 1845, Cambridge.
**Levi Washburn Leonard*, *A. M.; S. T. D.* 1849, Bridgewater.
*William H. Moulton, Boston.
*Gayton Pickman Osgood, *A. M.; M. C.* Andover.
**Edmund Quincy Sewell*, *A. M.* Marblehead.
*Pelham Winslow Warren, *A. M.* Plymouth.
**John Lee Watson*, *A. M.; S. T. D.* Columbia 1852, Boston.

1816

*Benjamin G. Allston, Charleston, S. C.
*John Vaughan Apthorp, *A. M.* Boston.
*William Howard Gardiner, *A. M.* Boston.
*Doddridge Crocker Hichborn, *A. M.* Charleston, S. C.
*John C. Jones, Boston.
*¶Samuel Philips Newman, *A. M.;* Princ. State Normal S. Barre; Prof. Anc. Lang. and Class. Lit., Prof. Rhet. and Orat. Bowd. Coll. Hanover, N. H.
*¶*Oliver William Bourn Peabody*, *A. M.; LL. B.* 1822; Prof. Eng. Lit. Jefferson Coll. (La.); Memb. Mass. Hist. Soc. Boston.
*Joseph Augustus Peabody, *A. M.* Salem.
*Henry Bromfield Pearson, *A. M.* Andover.
*¶Samuel Perry, *D. M.* also *G. M.* New Bedford.

FRONT ROOM—NEW CLUB

*Augustus Thorndike, *A. M.; D. Ml*, also *G. Ml*, Boston.
*Henry Artemas Ward, *A. M.; M. D.* 1832; *L. P. C.* Boston.
*William Rounsville Peirce Washburn, *LL. B.* 1820, Middleborough.
*¶Joseph Willard, *A. M.; LL. B.* 1820, Cambridge.

K. S. T.

1816

*George Baker, *A. M.; M. D.* 1820, Dedham.
*John James Devereux, 1849; *A. M.* 1850, Salem.
*Thomas H. Everett, Boston.
**William Bourn Oliver Peabody*, *A. M.; S. T. D.* 1842, Springfield.
*Jonathan Greeley Stevenson, *A. M.; M. D.* 1826, Boston.
**William Ware*, *A. M.* Brookline.

1817

*Daniel Heyward Brailsford, *A. M.* 1827, Charleston, S. C.
*¶Samuel Atkins Eliot, *A. M.*; Div. S. 1820; Treasurer; Fellow Am. Acad.; *M. C.* Boston.
*¶*Benjamin Fessenden*, *A. M.* Sandwich.
*Wyllys Lyman, Yale 1817; *LL. B.* 1820, Hartford, Vt.
*¶*Samuel Joseph May*, *A. M.* Boston.
*Samuel H. Myers, Richmond, Va.
*¶Robert Schuyler, *A. M.* Rhinebeck, N. Y.
*Oliver Sheafe, *A. M.; L. P. C.* Portsmouth, N. H.
*¶*Thomas Russell Sullivan*, *A. M.; D. Ml*, Boston.
*¶Charles Henry Warren, *A. M.* Plymouth.
*¶Francis William Winthrop, *D. M.* also *G. M.* Boston.

K. S. T.

1817

*William Ferdinand Carey, Chelsea.
*Joseph Coolidge, *A. M.* Boston.
*Caleb Cushing, *A. M.; LL. D.* 1852; Tutor; Overseer; Fellow Am. Acad.; Memb. Mass.

Hist. Soc.; Just. Supr. Court Mass.; Attorney-Gen. U. S.; *M. C.;* U. S. Comm. to conclude peace with China; U. S. Min. Plen. China, Spain, Newburyport.

*George Barrell Emerson, *A. M.; LL. D.* 1859, Brown 1858; Tutor; Fellow Am. Acad.; Memb. Mass. Hist. Soc. Boston.

*Sylvanus Lazell Mitchell, Bridgewater.

*John Larkin Payson, *A. M.* Charlestown.

*Samuel Soley, Charlestown.

*Samuel Perkins Spear, Boston.

1818

*John Hooker Ashmun, *Hon. Mem.* 1830; *A. M.;* Royal Prof. Law, Cambridge.

*¶Francis Brinley, *A. M.* 1827, Boston.

*William Augustus Carson, Charleston, S. C.

*George Chase, Portland, Me.

**Philander Chase,* Worthington, O.

*Ralph Emms Elliott, *M. D.* 1824, Coll. Phys. and Surg. N. Y. 1821, Beaufort, S. C.

*¶John Everett, *A. M.;* Tutor Transylvania Univ. (Ky.) Boston.

*Thomas Gadsden, Charleston, S. C.

*Joseph Gilman, *D. M'l,* Philadelphia, Pa.

*Nathaniel Hathaway, *L. P. C.* New Bedford.

*Joshua Henshaw Hayward, *A. M.; M. D.* 1821, Boston.

*Bela Latham, Lyme, N. H.

*Thomas McCullock, Kennebunk, Me.

*¶Grenville Mellen, *Hon. Mem.; D. M.* Portland, Me.

*Richard Morris, *Hon. Mem.; A. M.* Yale, New York, N. Y.

*William Parsons, *A. M.* Boston.

*Edward Robertson, Virginia.

*¶Winslow Warren Sever, *A. M.* 1823; *G. M.* Kingston.

*Robert Waight, Beaufort, S. C.

*Charles Walker, Tutor, and Librarian Transylvania Univ. (Ky.) Concord, N. H.

*Robert Breck Garven Williams, *A. M.* Boston.

1819

*Thomas Leaming Caldwell, *A. M.*; Tutor Transylvania Univ. Philadelphia, Pa.
*Charles Shirley Carter, Pr. Wm. Co., Va.
*¶Thomas Savage Clay, *A. M.*; *G. M.* Medford.
*¶Thomas Bulfinch Coolidge, also Yale 1819, *A. M.* Boston.
*John R. Dall, Baltimore, Md.
*¶Edward Dorr, *A. M.* Roxbury.
*James Cutler Dunn, *A. M.* Boston.
*Samuel Taylor Gilman, *A. M.*; *L. P. C.* Exeter, N. H.
*John Haslett, *A. M.*; *M. D.* Penn. 1822, Brooklyn, N. Y.
*¶Edward Ellenborough Law, New London, Ct.
*Charles Carter Lee, *A. M.* Alexandria, Va.
*Charles Lyman, *A. M.*; *D. M'l*, Boston.

K. S. T.

1819

*Sidney Brooks, *A. M.* Boston.
*Horace Gray, *A. M.* Boston.
*Nathaniel Leech Hooper, also Yale 1821, *A. M.* Marblehead.
*Winslow Lewis, *A. M.*; *M. D.* 1822, Boston.
*Phillips Payson, Charlestown.
*Stephen Clarendon Phillips, *A. M.*; *M. C.* Salem.
George Henry Snelling, also Yale 1819, *A. M.* Boston.
*Henry Upham, *A. M.*; *D. M.* Brookfield.

1820

*¶Joseph Thornton Adams, *A. M.*; *G. M.* Boston.
*Thomas John Bowie, Georgetown, D. C.
*John Sanford Dart, Charleston, S. C.
*¶James Ferdinand Deering, *A. M.* Westbrook, Me.
*Archibald Dunbar, Natchez, Miss.
William Henry Furness, *A. M.*; *S. T. D.* 1847, Medford.
*David Priestley Hall, *A. M.* Pomfret, Ct.

*¶Alfred Woodward Haven, *A. M.* Portsmouth, N. H.
*¶Isaac Lothrop Hedge, *A. M.* Plymouth.
*¶George Barber Osborn, *A. M.* Boston.
*¶CHARLES PAINE, *A. M.; Gov. Vt.; L. P. C.* Williamstown, Vt.
*William George Read, *A. M.; LL. D.* Georgetown 1842; *D. M'l*, Charleston, S. C.
*¶John Rogers, *A. M.* Boston.
*¶*Stephen Schuyler*, *A. M.* 1845, Rhinebeck, N. Y.
*William Rufus Smith, Natchez, Miss.
*William M. Steuart, Georgetown, D. C.
*¶Francis Henry Williams, *A. M.* Boston.

K. S. T.

1820

*Thaddeus Bowman Bigelow, *A. M.* Cambridge.
*Frederick Augustus Cobb, *A. M.* 1824, Portland, Me.
*Gideon Tucker, Salem.
*Adolphus Eugene Watson, *A. M.* Cambridge.

1821

*ROBERT WOODWARD BARNWELL, *A. M.;* Pres. S. Carolina Coll.; *M. C.;* Senator U. S. Beaufort, S. C.
*Allard Henry Belin, *A. M.* Charleston, S. C.
*Horton Bethune, *A. M.; M. D.* Columbia 1829, Charleston, S. C.
*William Parker Coffin, Charleston, S. C.
*George Minot Dexter, Boston.
*¶David Wood Gorham, *M. D.* 1824; *L. P. C.* Canandaigua, N. Y.
*Robert Marion Gourdin, *M. D.* Coll. Phys. and Surg. N. Y. 1824, Pineville, S. C.
*John Gaillard Keith Gourdin, Pineville, S. C.
*¶George Johonnot Hubbard, Boston.
*Francis Cabot Lowell, *A. M.* 1825, Boston.
*¶Samuel Hall Lyon, *D. M.* Baltimore, Md.
*Joseph Manigault, Charleston, S. C.
**Mellish Irving Motte*, *A. M.* Charleston, S. C.
*Henry Manly Neyle, Charleston, S. C.

*¶William Foster Otis, _A. M.; D. M'l,_ also _G. M._ Boston.
*William H. Pope, Louisville, Ky.
*¶Benjamin Tyler Reed, Boston.
*¶Andrew Turnbull, Charleston, S. C.
*CHARLES WENTWORTH UPHAM, _A. M.; M. C._ Salem.

K. S. T.

1821

*John Lowell Gardner, _A. M._ Boston.
*George Williams Pratt, _A. M._ Boston.

1822

*Larz Anderson, _A. M._ 1858; _D. M'l,_ Louisville, Ky.
*¶CHARLES GORDON ATHERTON, _A. M.; M. C.;_ Senator U. S. Amherst, N. H.
*Oliver Bronson, _Hon. Mem.; A. M._ Yale, New York, N. Y.
*¶Jephthah A. T. Bynum, Alexandria, La.
*¶Thomas Farr Capers, _A. M._ Charleston, S. C.
*¶William Putnam Endicott, Salem.
*¶George Fox, _A. M._ Philadelphia, Pa.
*¶Edward Jackson Lowell, _A. M.; LL. B._ 1825, Boston.
*George M. Morris, _Hon. Mem._ Charleston, S. C.
*Henry Bromfield Rogers, _A. M._ Boston.
*¶Norman Seaver, _A. M.; D. M._ Boston.
*¶Henry Stout, Dover, Del.
*Daniel Wikoff, Opelousas, La.
*William Yates, _M. D._ Penn. 1825; _L. P. C._ Charleston, S. C.

K. S. T.

1822

*_Timothy Darling,_ Henniker, N. H.
*Charles Phelps Huntington, Hadley.
*Richard Bennet Granger Mitchell, Baltimore, Md.
*Henry Harding Penniman, New Braintree.
*John Holbrook Richards, _A. M.; M. D._ 1825, Dedham.

*James Sullivan,	Boston.
*Alexander Thomas, *A. M.; M. D.* 1827,	Boston.
*Ebenezer Torrey, *A. M.*	Lancaster.

1823

*¶William Amory, 1845; *A. M.* 1845,	Boston.
*Samuel Parkman Blake, 1841; *A. M.* 1841,	Boston.
*¶Frederick Bronson, 1824; *A. M.* 1848,	New York, N. Y.
*Thomas Jefferson Bryan, 1843; *A. M.* 1843,	Philadelphia, Pa.
*David Bullock,	Richmond, Va.
*¶George Henry Calvert, 1855,	Pr. Geo. Co., Md.
*Charles Carroll, 1855,	Baltimore, Md.
*¶Charles Chapin, 1855; *M. D.* 1826,	Brattleboro, Vt.
*¶Jacob Crowninshield,	Salem.
*John Atkinson Cunningham, 1850; *A. M.* 1850,	Richmond, Va.
*Robert Thomas Dunbar,	Natchez, Miss.
*JAMES DANDRIDGE HALYBURTON, 1850; *A. M.* 1850; Judge U. S. Dist. Court Va.	Richmond, Va.
*¶Charles Carroll Harper,	Baltimore, Md.
*¶Charles Thompson Haskell, 1855,	Charleston, S. C.
*Phineas Miller Kollock, *M. D.* Penn. 1826,	Savannah, Ga.
*David Minge,	Richmond, Va.
¶George Peabody, 1843; *A. M.* 1843; *D. M'l,* also *G. M.*	Salem.
*¶Russell Sturgis, 1845; *A. M.* 1845; *L. P. C.,* also *G. M'l,*	Boston.
Warner T. Taliaferro,	Glo'ster Co., Va.
*Edward Thornton Tayloe, 1854,	Washington, D. C.

K. S. T.

1823

*John Adams, 1873,	Quincy.
*Henry Grafton Chapman, 1841; *A. M.* 1841,	Boston.
*Martin Gay, 1841; *A. M.* 1841; *M. D.* 1826,	Hingham.

1824

*¶*William Hazzard Wigg Barnwell,*	Beaufort, S. C.
*John Francis Bingaman,	Natchez, Miss.
*¶Edward Blake, *A. M.*	Boston.
¶William Boott,	Boston.
*Charles Henry Carter,	Fauquier Co., Va.
*Alexander Clarke Dunbar,	Natchez, Miss.
**Stephen Elliott, A. M.*	Beaufort, S. C.
*¶John Henry Gray, *A. M.*	Boston.
Horatio Nelson Lloyd,	Alexandria, D. C.
*¶William Edward Payne, *A. M.*	Boston.
*Charles Gideon Putnam, *A. M.; M. D.* 1827; *L. P. C.*	Salem.
*Daniel Clark Relf, *A. M.; D. M'l,*	New Orleans, La.
*Nathaniel Silsbee, *A. M.* 1862; Treasurer,	Salem.
*Calvin Stephen Smith,	Natchez, Miss.
*Josiah Smith,	St. Augustine, Fla.
*John H. Wickham, *LL. D.* 1815,	Richmond, Va.

K. S. T.

1824

*Samuel Adams Cooper, *A. M.*	Salem.
*Rufus Dawes,	Boston.
*George Bucknam Dorr, 1866,	Boston.
*John Thomas Phillip Dumont, *A. M.*	Boston.
*Benjamin S. Gibbes,	Charleston, S. C.
*Walter Izard,	Charleston, S. C.
*Thomas Lowndes,	Charleston, S. C.
*William Pratt, *A. M.* 1828,	Boston.
*Charles Church Chandler Tucker,	Boston.
*Henry Samuel Tudor,	Hartford, Ct.
*William Wilson Wheelwright,	Boston.

1825

*James M. Alston,	Clark Co., Ala.
*Hilary Breton Cenas, *A. M.; L. P. C.*	New Orleans, La.

*¶Jonathan Chapman, *A. M.* — Boston.
*¶*Francis Cunningham, G. M.* — Boston.
*¶William Dwight, — Springfield.
*Stephen Elliott, *A. M.* — Charleston, S. C.
*Joshua Francis Fisher, *A. M.* — Philadelphia, Pa.
*¶William M. Garrow, — Mobile, Ala.
*Charles D. Manigault, — Charleston, S. C.
*Peter Manigault, — Charleston, S. C.
*¶William Miller, *D. M.* — Philadelphia, Pa.
*John G. North, — Charleston, S. C.
*¶Allyne Otis, *A. M.* — Boston.
*Robert Dow Percy, *L. P. C.* — St. Francisville, La.
**Edward Goldsborough Prescott, A. M.* — Boston.
**Paul Trapier, S. T. D.* 1867; *D. M'l,* — Charleston, S. C.
*¶George Augustus Beverly Walker, *D. M'l, D. M.*, also *G. M.* — Augusta, Ga.
*¶Charles Willing, *M. D.* Penn. 1828, — Philadelphia, Pa.

K. S. T.

1825

*CHARLES FRANCIS ADAMS, *A. M.; LL. D.* 1864, Yale 1872; Overseer; Memb. Mass. Hist. Soc. and Am. Philos. Soc.; Vice-Pres. and Pres. Am. Acad.; Hon. Memb. Soc. Antiq. London; *M. C.;* U. S. Min. Plen. Gt. Britain, — Boston.
*Edward Dewey, — Boston.
*Benjamin B. Fessenden, — Boston.
*Charles Phineas Foster, — Boston.
**Samuel Kirkland Lothrop, A. M.; S. T. D.* 1852, — Boston.
*John Hancock Richardson, *A. M.* — Newton.
*Edward Rundlet, *M. D.* 1829, — Portsmouth, N. H.
*George Sheafe, — Portsmouth, N. H.
*George Edward Winthrop, *A. M.* — Boston.

1826

*Jerome Napoleon Bonaparte, *D. M'l,* — Baltimore, Md.
*Robert N. Carnan, — Baltimore, Md.

LONG ROOM—OLD CLUB

*Joseph Heatley Cheves,	Philadelphia, Pa.
*Charles J. Hunt,	Boston.
*Adolphus Peter Jouve, *A. M.* 1831; *L. P. C.*	Havana, Cuba.
*George Caspar Jouve,	Havana, Cuba.
*Edward Carrington Marshall,	Richmond, Va.
*William H. Morgan,	New Orleans, La.
*James L. Murray,	Baltimore, Md.
*Edward North, *M. D.* Coll. So. Carolina, 1829,	Charleston, S. C.
*George Franklin Turner, *M. D.* 1830,	Richmond, Va.

K. S. T.

1826

*George Atherton,	Amherst, N. H.
*Benjamin Cox, *A. M.; M. D.* 1829,	Salem.
*Charles Russell Lowell, *A. M.*	Boston.
**John Charles Phillips,*	Boston.
*Stephen Minot Weld, *A. M.*	Lancaster.

1827

*Thomas Alston,	Georgetown, S. C.
*¶Benjamin Varnum Crowninshield, *D. M.*, also *G. M.*	Salem.
*¶Thomas Kemper Davis, *A. M.; G. M'l,*	Boston.
¶Epes Sargent Dixwell, *Hon. Mem.; A. M.*	Boston.
*¶Francis Dwight, *D. M'l,* also *G. M.*	Springfield.
*¶Thomas Dwight, *L. P. C.*	Boston.
*¶Edward William Hook, *Hon. Mem.; M. D.* 1832,	Castine, Me.
**Alfred Lee, A. M.; S. T. D.* 1860, Trinity (Conn.) 1841, Kenyon (O.) 1841, Hobart (N. Y.) 1841, Delaware 1877; Bishop Del. 1887,	Norwich, Ct.
*¶George Augustus Meredith, *A. M.*	Raleigh, N. C.
*¶Charles Cushing Paine, *A. M.*	Boston.
¶William Powell Perkins, *A. M.*	Boston.
*Edmund Quincy, *A. M.;* Overseer; Fellow Am. Acad.; Memb. Mass. Hist. Soc. and Am. Philos. Soc.	Boston.

*William Henry Roosevelt, New York, N. Y.
¶James Gillespie Rowe, Newbern, N. C.
**John Turner Sargent, A. M.* Boston.
*¶William Schuyler, Rhinebeck, N. Y.

K. S. T.

1827

*Frederick Hall Bradlee, Boston.
*Francis Dana, 1867; *A. M.* 1831, Cambridge.
*Simon Gratz, Philadelphia, Pa.
*William Bradbury Kingsbury, Roxbury.
*James Savage, Philadelphia, Pa.
*Nathaniel Burger Shaler, 1870; *M. D.* 1829, Newport, Ky.
*Arnold Francis Welles, *Hon. Mem.* 1832; *A. M.* Boston.

1828

*¶Arthur Howson Hooe Bernard, Fredericksb'g, Va.
*Frederick Dabney, *A. M.* Fayal, Azores.
*Joseph Willard Dana, Cambridge.
*Charles Chauncy Emerson, *Hon. Mem.; A. M., LL. B.* 1832, Boston.
*¶Robert Gilmor, Baltimore, Md.
*Patrick Grant, *A. M.* Boston.
**John Singleton Copley Green, A. M.*, also Racine, 1854; *M. D.* 1831, Boston.
*James Jackson, *A. M.; M. D.* 1834, Boston.
*¶Francis Caleb Loring, *A. M.; L. P. C.* Boston.
*Henry Swasey McKean, *Hon. Mem.* 1835; *A. M.;* Tutor, Cambridge.
*¶Charles Tracy Murdoch, *A. M.; LL. B.* 1832, Havana, Cuba.
*¶William Phillips, Boston.
**Robert Charles Winthrop, A. M.; LL. D.* 1855, Bowd. 1849, Kenyon (O.) 1851, Cambr. 1874; Overseer; Pres. Mass. Hist. Soc.; Fellow Am. Acad; Memb. Am. Philos. Soc., Kon. Nord. Oldskr.-Selsk. (Copenhagen); Hon. Memb.

Soc. Antiq. London, Roy. Hist. Soc. (London), Inst. Hist. Geogr. Ethnogr. Brasil.; *M. C.* (Speaker); Senator U. S.; *D. M'l*, also *G. M.* Boston.

K. S. T.

1828

*James Henry Blake, Boston.
**George Chapman*, Boston.
*Samuel Fulton, Alexandria, La.
*JOHN JAMES GILCHRIST, *LL. D.* 1856 Dart. 1852; Just. and Ch. Just. Supr. Court N. H.; Judge U. S. Court of Claims. Charlestown, N. H.
*Eugene Thomas Whittell Moore, Natchez, Miss.
**William Gray Swett, A. M.* Boston.
*John Parker Tarbell, *A. M.* Cambridge.
*Charles Joseph Taylor, Boston.
*Benjamin Duick Whitney, *G. M.* Boston.

1829

**William Henry Channing*, Boston.
*¶Francis Boardman Crowninshield, *Hon. Mem.* 1830, 1843; *A. M.* 1843; Fellow, Boston.
*BENJAMIN ROBBINS CURTIS, *LL. B.* 1832; *LL. D.* 1852; Brown 1857; Fellow; Fellow Am. Acad.; Memb. Mass. Hist. Soc.; Just. Supr. Court U. S. Cambridge.
*¶*Charles Fay, A. M.* Cambridge.
William Gray, *A. M.* Boston.
*¶Solomon Martin Jenkins, *M. D.* Penn. 1831, Easton, Md.
*¶Edward Patrick Milliken, *D. M'l*, Charleston, S. C.
*¶*Isaac Edward Morse, M. C.; D. M'l*, New Orleans, La.
*¶Benjamin Peirce, *A. M.* 1833; *LL. D.* 1867, Univ. N. C. 1847; Tutor; Coll. Prof. Math. and Nat. Philos.; Perkins Prof. Astron. and Math.; Fellow Am. Acad., Royal Soc. London, Edinb.; Memb. Am. Philos. Soc., Kön. Ges. Wiss. Göttingen; Supt. U. S. Coast Surv. Cambridge.

*George William Phillips, *Hon. Mem.* Boston.
*Benjamin Morgan Saul, *Hon. Mem.* New Orleans, La.
Charles Storer Storrow, *Hon. Mem.* Boston.
*William Watson Sturgis, Boston.
*¶Ezra Weston, *A. M.; LL. B.* 1832; *L. P. C.* Duxbury.

K. S. T.

1829

Edward Linzee Cunningham, *A. M.; M. D.* 1832; *G. M.* Boston.
*Nathaniel Foster Derby, Salem.
*George Humphrey Devereux, *A. M.* Salem.
*George Gardner, *A. M.* Boston.
Oliver Wendell Holmes, *A. M.* (Hon.) 1889; *M. D.* 1836; *LL. D.* 1880, Edinb. 1886; Litt. D. Cambr. 1886; *D. C. L.* Oxford 1886; Parkman Prof. Anat. and Physiol., and Prof. Emeritus; Dean Med. S.; Overseer; Prof. Anat. and Physiol. Dart. Coll.; Vice-Pres. Am. Acad.; Memb. Mass. Hist. Soc., and Am. Philos. Soc. Boston.
*Washington Lazarus, Wilmington, N. C.
Samuel May, A. M. Leicester.
**Chandler Robbins, A. M.; S. T. D.* 1855, Roxbury.
*Howard Sargent, *A. M.; M. D.* 1832, Boston.
*James Edward Sheafe, Portsmouth, N. H.
*Joshua Holyoke Ward, *A. M.; LL. B.* 1832. Salem.

1830

*Thomas Coffin Amory, *A. M.* Boston.
*¶John Bryant, *A. M.; D. M'l,* Boston.
*Bernard Fitzhugh Carter, *Hon. Mem.* Fauquier Co., Va.
*Charles Du Bignon, *Hon. Mem.* Savannah, Ga.
*Horace Sprague Eustis, *A. M.* 1838, O. P. Comfort, Va.
*George James Foster, *A. M.* Boston.
*Robert Hallowell Gardiner, Gardiner, Me.
*Benjamin Gwinn Harris, *Hon. Mem.* St. Mary's Co., Md.
*Robert William Hooper, *Hon. Mem.; A. M.; M. D.* 1836; Fellow Am. Acad. Marblehead.

*Isaac Appleton Jewett, Columbus, Ohio.
*¶JOHN BOZMAN KERR, *A. M.; M. C.; L. P. C.* Easton, Md.
*Henry Winthrop Sargent, *A. M.* Boston.
¶John Osborne Sargent, *G. M.* Boston.
*Theodore Sedgwick, *Hon. Mem.* Stockbridge.
**Theodore William Snow, A. M.* Boston.
*William Henry Stiles, *Hon. Mem.* Savannah, Ga.
*CHARLES SUMNER, *LL. B.* 1834; *LL. D.* 1859, Yale 1856, Amherst, 1856; Fellow Am. Acad.; Memb. Am. Philos. Soc., and Mass. Hist. Soc.; Senator U. S. Boston.
*Charlemagne Tower, *A. M.* Paris, N. Y.
*¶Joseph Barney Williams, *A. M.* Baltimore, Md.

K. S. T.

1830

*Joseph Lyman, *A. M.; D. M.* Northampton.
*James Swan Sullivan, *M. D.* Boston.

1831

*Thomas Gold Appleton, *A. M.* 1877, Boston.
*Francis Boott, *A. M.* Boston.
*¶Frederick William Brune, *A. M.* Baltimore, Md.
*Francis Lowell Dutton, *LL. B.* 1834, Boston.
*¶Henry Frederick Friese, *A. M.* 1832; *G. M.* Baltimore, Md.
*William Cabot Gorham, *Hon. Mem.* Boston.
*¶Robert Habersham, *L. P. C.* Savannah, Ga.
*Herman Brimmer Inches, *A. M.; M. D.* 1834, Boston.
*John George McKean, *Hon. Mem.* 1835, New York, N. Y.
*Wendell Phillips, *LL. B.* 1834; *D. M'l, G. M'l,* Boston.
George Cheyne Shattuck, *A. M.; M. D.* 1835; Prof. Clin. Med.; Hersey Prof. Theo. and Pract. Med.; Dean Med. S.; Prof. Physiol. and Instit. Med. Trinity Coll. (Conn.); Fellow Am. Acad. Boston.
*Francis Henry Silsbee, Salem.
*John T. S. Sullivan, *Hon. Mem.* Boston.
*¶Charles Henry Tilghman, *A. M.* 1839, Easton, Md.
*Abraham Rand Thompson, Charlestown.

K. S. T.

1831

*Charles Harris, Boston.

*John Lothrop Motley, *Ph. D.* Gröningen; *Litt. D* Univ. N. Y.; *LL. D.* 1860, Univ. City N. Y. 1858, Cambr. 1861, Leyden 1872; *J. C. D.* Oxford 1860; Memb. Mass. Hist. Soc.; Fellow Am. Acad.; Memb. Am. Philos. Soc.; Maatsch. Nederl. Letterk. (Leyden), Hist. Gezelsch. Utrecht; Hon. Member Society Antiq. London, Roy. Soc. Hist. (London); Memb. Kon. Nederl. Inst. Wetensch. (Amsterdam); Cor. Member Acad. Imp. Sci. (St. Petersburg); Cor. Memb., and For. Assoc. Acad. Sci. Mor. et Pol. (Institut de France); U. S. Min. Plen. Austria, Gt. Britain, Boston.

*Samuel Wigglesworth, *A. M.; M. D.* 1834; *D. M.* Boston.

1832

*¶Horatio Bigelow, 1866, Cambridge.

*¶Richard Miller Chapman, *A. M.; LL. B.* 1836, Boston.

*¶George Caspar Crowninshield, Boston.

*John Warren Gorham, *A. M.; M. D.* 1837, Boston.

*Rhett Jacob Motte, *M. D.* Med. Coll. S. C. Charleston, S. C.

*¶*John Parkman,* Brighton.

*¶Samuel Parkman Shaw, *A. M.; L. P. C.* Boston.

*John Boardman Silsbee, *Hon. Mem.* 1832, Salem.

*¶JOSEPH STEVENS BUCKMINSTER THACHER, Just. Supr. Court Miss.; *D. M'l,* Boston.

*¶Alanson Tucker, Derry, N. H.

*James Sullivan Warren, *A. M.* Boston.

K. S. T.

1832

*James Augustus Dorr, Boston.

**Oliver Capen Everett, A. M.* Boston.

*Henry Waring Latane Temple, Essex Co., Va.

MEMBERS OF THE P. C. SINCE THE UNION OF THE P. C. AND K. S. T.

1833

*Gervais Baillio,	Alexandria, La.
George Inglis Crafts, *A. M.* 1837,	Charleston, S. C.
*William Dehon, 1834; *L. P. C.*	Boston.
*Henry Yancey Gray, *Hon. Mem.*	Charleston, S. C.
*John Joy,	Boston.
Waldo Higginson, *A. M.* 1856,	Cambridge.
*Charles Jackson,	Boston.
*Francis Eben Oliver,	Boston.
*Charles Henry Peirce, *A. M.; M. D.* 1836,	Cambridge.
*Fletcher Webster, *D. M'l,*	Boston.
Charles Alfred Welch, *G. M'l,*	Boston.

1834

*Gideon Forrester Barstow, *A. M.; M. D.* 1837,	Salem.
*Edward Darley Boit, 1844; *A. M.* 1844; *LL. B.* 1844,	Boston.
**Henry Burroughs*, 1835, *Hon. Mem.; S. T. D.* Trin. 1876,	Boston.
*Frederick Dwight, 1863,	Springfield.
*James Tilghman Earle, *Hon. Mem.* 1863,	Centreville, Md.
*Drausin Baltazar Labranche,	St. Chas. Par., La.
*Rufus Bigelow Lawrence,	Lowell.
*Samuel Parkman, *A. M.; M. D.* 1838; Fellow Am. Acad.; *G. M'l,*	Boston.
*John Turner Welles Sargent, 1835,	Boston.
**William Vincent Thacher, A. M.*	Boston.
*Henry Constantine Wayne,	Savannah, Ga.
*Charles Henry Wheelwright, 1875; *M. D.* 1837; *D. M'l,*	Boston.

*Robert Wickliffe, Lexington, Ky.
JOSEPH HARTWELL WILLIAMS, 1835; *LL. B.* 1837; Gov. Maine; *L. P. C.* Augusta, Me.

1835

William Henry Allen, *A. M.; D. M'l,* New Bedford.
William Frederick Frick, *L. P. C.* Baltimore, Md.
Charles Horatio Gates, 1873, Montreal, L. C.
*Daniel Jones, Nantucket.
*Nemèse Harmogène Labranche, St. Chas. Par., La.
*Amos Adams Lawrence, Treasurer; Overseer; Memb. Mass. Hist. Soc. Boston.
Charles Henry Parker, Boston.
*Thomas Pinckney Rutledge, *D. M'l,* Charleston, S. C.

1836

*Samuel Cabot, *A. M.; M. D.* 1839; Fellow Am. Acad. Boston.
*John William Tudor Gardiner, Gardiner, Me.
John Thompson Gray, *A. M.* 1871; *LL. B.* 1839; *D. M'l,* Louisville, Ky.
William Neyle Habersham, Savannah, Ga.
William Minot, *LL. B.* 1840, Boston.
*Grenville Tudor Phillips, *L. P. C.* Boston.
*John Harleston Read, *A. M.* Charleston, S. C.
Samuel Gray Ward, *A. M.* Boston.

1837

*Simon Forrester Barstow, *LL. B.* 1841, Salem.
*Richard Henry Dana, *A. M.; LL. B.* 1839; *LL. D.* 1866, Hobart (N. Y.) 1853; Instr. Elocution; Overseer; Memb. Mass. Hist. Soc.; Fellow Am. Acad. Boston.
*Louis Salvador Fellowes, Havana, Cuba.
William Whitwell Greenough, Boston.
*Samuel Tenney Hildreth, Instructor Elocution, Gloucester.

LONG ROOM—NEW CLUB

*Christopher Columbus Holmes, *A. M.; M. D.* 1840; *L. P. C.* Kingston.
*Henry Hubbard, *A. M.; LL. B.* 1840; *D. M'l,* Charlestown, N. H.
*Joseph Alston Huger, Charleston, S. C.
*James Gales Seaton, Washington, D. C.
*Supply Clap Thwing, *Hon. Mem.* Roxbury.
*John Francis Tuckerman, *A. M.; M. D.* 1841; *L. P. C.* Boston.
*William Pinckney Williams, Baltimore, Md.
*Edward Pinckney Williams, Baltimore, Md.

1838

*Gerard Bond Bate, Louisville, Ky.
*Wendell Thornton Davis, Greenfield.
*James Barnwell Heyward, *D. M'l,* Charleston, S. C.
*William Henry Heyward, Charleston, S. C.
JAMES RUSSELL LOWELL, *A. M.; LL. B.* 1840; *J. C. D.* Oxford 1873; *LL. D.* 1884, Cambr. 1874, St. Andrews 1884, Edinb. 1884, Bologna 1888; Smith Prof. French and Span. Lang. and Lit. and Prof. Belles Lettres, and Smith Prof. Emeritus; Rector St. Andrews Univ.; Overseer; Fellow Am. Acad.; Memb. Mass. Hist. Soc., Am. Philos. Soc., and Real Acad. Española; Fellow Royal Soc. (Edinb.), and Royal Soc. Lit. (London); U. S. Min. Plen. Spain, Gt. Britain; *Hon. Mem.* 1857, Cambridge.
Thomas McLaughlin, *Hon. Mem.; LL. B.* 1839, Columbia, Miss.
*WILLIAM PRESTON, *Hon. Mem.; LL. B.* 1838; Min. Plen. Spain; *M. C.* Louisville, Ky.
*Benjamin Garden Pringle, *Hon. Mem.* Charleston, S. C.
*Benjamin Smith Rotch, *A. M.* 1870; *L. P. C.* New Bedford.
William James Rotch, *A. M.* 1870, New Bedford.
William Wetmore Story, *A. M.; LL. B.* 1840; *D. C. L.* Oxford 1887; Prof. Accad. Sta. Cecilia (Rome), Prof. Accad. Quiriti, Accad. Arcadi (Rome); Fellow Am. Acad.; Memb. Mass. Hist. Soc.; Chev. de l'Ordre de François I[e]. Cambridge.

1839

Loring Henry Austin, *A. M.* Cambridge.
*Kirk Boott, *G. M'l,* Cambridge.
*George William Christy, *D. M'l,* New Orleans, La.
*Joseph Lewis Danforth, Louisville, Ky.
*Enos Williams Dean, Boston.
Samuel Eliot, *A. M.; A. M.* (Hon.) Trinity (Conn.) 1857; *LL. D.* 1880, Columbia 1863; Overseer; Headmaster Girls' High S. Boston; Brownell Prof. Hist. and Polit. Sci., and Pres. Trinity Coll. (Conn.); Memb. Mass. Hist. Soc.; Fellow Am. Acad.; Supt. Pub. Schools Boston, Cambridge.
*Romuald Labranche, *L. P. C.* Jeff. Par., La.
*James Johnson Moore, Harrodsburg, Ky.
*Thomas Snead, *D. M'l,* Louisville, Ky.
*Richard Cleveland Stillwell, *A. M.* 1846; *M. D.* 1843; Berks. Med. Coll. Lancaster.

1840

*Henry Bryant, *A. M.; M. D.* 1843; Fellow Am. Acad. Boston.
James Elliot Cabot, *LL. B.* 1845; *LL. D.* 1886; Overseer; Fellow Am. Acad. Boston.
*John Francis Heath, *A. M.; D. M'l,* Petersburg, Va.
*Nathaniel Dean Hubbard, Charlestown, N. H.
*James Lawrence, *A. M.; L. P. C.* Boston.
**Joseph Coolidge Shaw*, *A. M.* Boston.
Edward Holker Welch, *A. M.; LL. B.* 1846; Adj. Prof. French, Prefect of Studies, and Prof. German Georgetown Univ. (D. C.) Boston.

1841

*Henry Fowle Durant, 1842, *L. P. C.* Boston.
*William Addison Fitzhugh, Pittsburgh, Pa.
*William Henry Orne, Milton, Me.
Edward Newton Perkins, *A. M.; D. M'l,* Boston.
*Francis Morgan Rotch, Louisville, N. Y.

1842

*Francis Henry Appleton, *LL. B.* 1845, Boston.
*James Greenough, Boston.
*Chauvet Edmund La Beaume, St. Louis, Mo.
George Theodore Lyman, *D. M'l,* Boston.
Benjamin White Nichols, *A. M.; LL. B.* 1845; *L. P. C.* Boston.
Stephen Henry Phillips, *LL. B.* 1844; Attorney-Gen., Min. Finance, Min. Foreign Affairs Hawaiian Islands, Salem.
*George Edward Rice, *A. M.; LL. B.* 1845, Boston.
*Samuel Conch Robinson, Richmond, Va.
*Alfred Rodman, New Bedford.
*William Logan Rodman, New Bedford.
*David Sears, *A. M.* 1852, Boston.
Frederick Sheld, New York, N. Y.

1843

*Francis L. Lee, *A. M.; L. P. C.,* also *G. M'l,* Boston.
*Charles Callahan Perkins, *A. M.;* Fellow Am. Acad.; Memb. Mass. Hist. Soc.; Cor. Member Acad. Inscrip. et Belles Lettres (Institut de France), *D. M'l,* Boston.
Thomas Handasyde Perkins, Boston.
*William Crowninshield Rogers, Salem.
Frederick Richard Sears, *A. M.* 1852; *L. P. C.* Boston.
*Osmond Tiffany, Baltimore, Md.
*George Cabot Ward, 1876, Boston.

1844

Henry Charles Chauncey, *A. M.* New York, N. Y.
James Gordon Clarke, *LL. B.* 1846, Nashua, N. H.
*Charles William Dabney, *D. M'l,* Fayal, Azores.
*Henry Tallman Davis, Boston.
*William Morris Hunt, 1868; *A. M.* 1864, Boston.
Leverett Saltonstall, *A. M.; LL. B.* 1847; Overseer; Memb. Mass. Hist. Soc. Salem.

*Joshua Clapp Stone, Boston.
Stephen Goodhue Wheatland, *L. P. C.* Salem.
Edward Wheelwright, *A. M.* Boston.

1845

*Frederick Cunningham, Boston.
Edward Dexter, *D. M'l*, also *G. M'l*, Boston.
John Rae Habersham, Savannah, Ga.
*Jonathan Hunt, Boston.
Edward Julius Pringle, *A. M.* Charleston, S. C.
Harrison Ritchie, *L. P. C.* Boston.
Quincy Adams Shaw, Boston.
William Shaw Tiffany, Baltimore, Md.

1846

Edward Bangs, *LL. B.* 1849; *G. M'l*, Watertown.
Francis Boott Brooks, *Hon. Mem.; LL. B.* 1846, Boston.
Francis James Child, *A. M.; Ph. D.* Göttingen 1854; *LL. D.* 1884; *L. H. D.* Columbia 1887; Instr. Rhet.; Tutor; Boylston Prof. Rhet. and Oratory; Prof. English; Fellow Am. Acad. Cambridge.
*John Amory Codman, Roxbury.
*Augustus Enoch Daniels, Danvers.
William Sohier Dexter, *LL. B.* 1848, Boston.
George Martin Lane, *A. M.* 1850; *Ph. D.* Göttingen 1851; Univ. Prof. Latin; Pope Prof. Latin; Fellow Am. Acad. Cambridge.
*Timothy Bigelow Lawrence, *A. M.* Boston.
Thomas R. Rodman, *L. P. C.* New Bedford.
*William Ellery Sedgwick, *D. M'l*, New York, N. Y.
*BERNARD CROSBY WHITMAN, Just. and Ch. Just. Supr. Court Nevada, Portland, Me.
*Henry Austin Whitney, *A. M.; G. M'l*, Boston.

1847

Charles Bruce, Halifax Co., Va.
WILLIAM CROWNINSHIELD ENDICOTT, *LL. D.* 1882; Overseer; Fellow; Memb. Mass. Hist. Soc.; Just. Supr. Court Mass.; Sec. War. U. S.; *L. P. C.* Salem.

*Joseph Peabody Gardner, *A. M.* Boston.
Augustine Heard, Ipswich.
*Roscoe Briggs Heath, *Hon. Mem.; LL. B.* 1848, Petersburg, Va.
*Colin Mackenzie, Baltimore, Md.
*Charles Henry Morrell, *D. M'l,* Havana, Cuba.
William Allen Neil, *A. M.* Columbus, Ohio
*William Cabell Rives, *Hon. Mem.* Virginia; *LL. B.* 1847, Richmond, Va.
Andrew Cunningham Wheelwright, *A. M.* Boston.

1848

Joseph Pringle Alston, *D. M'l,* Charleston, S. C.
*John David Hobson, *Hon. Mem.* Richmond, Va.
James Steuart Thorndike, *A. M.; LL. B.* 1850; *L. P. C.* Boston.
*George Peabody Tiffany, *A. M.* Baltimore, Md.
*Alexander Scammell Wadsworth, Washington, D. C.

1849

Jerome Napoleon Bonaparte, Baltimore, Md.
Martin Brimmer, Overseer; Fellow; Memb. Mass. Hist. Soc.; Fellow Am. Acad.; *D. M'l,* Boston.
*Arthur Bronson, *Hon. Mem.* New York, N. Y.
*Joseph Swett Coolidge, *L. P. C.*, also *G. M'l,* Boston.
Francis Hathaway, New Bedford.
Edward Jackson, Boston.
*Henry Elliott Johnston, Baltimore, Md.
Josiah Lee Johnston, Baltimore, Md.
Abbott Lawrence, *A. M.* 1853; *LL. B.* 1863; Memb. Mass. Hist. Soc. Boston.
James Edward Macfarland, *Hon. Mem.; LL. B.* 1849, Richmond, Va.
*John Stewart Walker, Richmond, Va.

1850

*Edmund Lincoln Baylies, *A. M.; L. P. C.* Boston.
Walter Channing Cabot, *D. M'l,* Boston.
John Lee Carroll, *Hon. Mem.;* Gov. Maryland, Baltimore, Md.
Thomas Jefferson Coolidge, *A. M.;* Overseer, Boston.

Robert Barnwell Fuller, Beaufort, S. C.
Horatio Hathaway, New Bedford.
*George Gardner Lowell, Boston.
*Charles Ridgely, Baltimore Co., Md.

1851

William Cutting, *Hon. Mem.* New York, N. Y.
*Francis Oliver Dabney, *L. P. C.* Fayal, Azores.
*William Nye Davis, 1852, *D. M'l,* Boston.
*Alexander Telfair Habersham, Savannah, Ga.
*Augustus Thorndike Perkins, *A. M.* 1860; *LL. B.* 1853; *Tr.* and *G. M'l,* Boston.

1852

*John Ellis Blake, *A. M.; M. D.* 1855, Boston.
Peter Chardon Brooks, *A. M.* 1871, Boston.
*John Sylvester Gardiner, Boston.
*William Edward Howe, *Hon. Mem.; LL. B.* 1853, Boston.
George Augustus Peabody, *LL. B.* 1855; *L. P. C.* Salem.
Edward Ellerton Pratt, *LL. B.* 1855, Boston.
*Paul Joseph Revere, Boston.
Knyvett Winthrop Sears, *A. M.* 1857, Boston.
Nathaniel Devereux Silsbee, *A. M.* Salem.
*George Brimmer Sohier, *A. M.* 1858, Boston.
Samuel Lothrop Thorndike, *A. M.; LL. B.* 1854; *D. M'l,* Beverly.

1853

Theodore Chase, *A. M.* Boston.
*William Henry Cunningham, *D. M'l,* Boston.
*William Frick, *Hon. Mem.* Baltimore, Md.
Charles Coolidge Pomeroy, *L. P. C.* Cincinnati, Ohio.
*James Noon Roosevelt, *Hon. Mem.* Union 1847; *A. M.* Union; *LL. B.* 1851, New York, N. Y.

1854

Edward Wainwright Codman, *A. M.* Boston.
*Brockholst Cutting, *Hon. Mem.* New York, N. Y.

BILLIARD ROOM—NEW CLUB

William Stanley Haseltine, *A. M.* 1858, Philadelphia, Pa.
Benjamin Joy Jeffries, *A. M.; M. D.* 1857; *Tr.* Boston.
*Gerard Walton Morris, *Hon. Mem.; LL. B.* 1854, New York, N. Y.
Robert Aloysius Renshaw, Caracas, Venez.
Charles Thorndike, *A. M.; LL. B.* 1857; *L. P. C.* Boston.
*William Thorndike, *A. M.; M. D.* 1857, Beverly.
Robert Charles Winthrop, 1855; *A. M.* 1858; Memb. Mass. Hist. Soc.; *D. M'l*, Boston.
Leonard Jarvis Wyeth, New York, N. Y.

1855

William Amory, Boston.
Samuel Parkman Blake, Roxbury.
Edward Ingersoll Browne, *LL. B.* 1857; *L. P. C., G. M'l*, Boston.
John Templeman Coolidge, *Hon. Mem.* Boston.
George Gordon Crocker, *A. M.* Taunton.
*John Gardner Cushing, *Hon. Mem.* Watertown.
George Dexter, Boston.
*Payson Perrin Ellis, Boston.
*Langdon Erving, *LL. B.* 1857, Baltimore, Md.
*Charles Frederick Lyman, *A. M.* 1866, Boston.
THEODORE LYMAN, *S. B.* 1858; Overseer; Fellow Am. Acad.; Memb. Mass. Hist. Soc., Nat. Acad. Sci.; Hon. M. N. Y. Acad. Sci.; *M. C.; D. M'l*, also *G. M'l*, Boston.
Willard Quincy Phillips, *A. M.; LL. B.* 1858, Cambridge.
*Samuel Ringgold Schley, *A. M.* Baltimore, Md.

1856

*Jacques Burkhardt, *Hon. Mem.* Neufchatel, Switz.
George Bigelow Chase, *A. M.;* Memb. Mass. Hist. Soc.; *L. P. C.* Boston.
*Arthur Amory Eckley, Boston.
*Charles Le Doux Elgee, *LL. B.* 1858, New Orleans, La.
Rowland Minturn Hall, New York, N. Y.
Leavitt Hunt, *Hon. Mem.; LL. B.* 1856; *J. U. D.* Heidelb. Brattleboro, Vt.
Edward Payson Jeffries, Boston.

William Powell Mason, *LL. B.* 1861, Boston.
Francis Blake Rice, *D. M'l*, Worcester.
Thomas Lindall Winthrop, *Hon. Mem.* Boston.

1857

*John Julius Pringle Alston, *D. M'l*, Charleston, S. C.
Shepherd Brooks, *A. M.* 1872, Boston.
John Langdon Dearborn, Exeter, N. H.
*Howard Dwight, *A. M.; L. P. C.* Brookline.
*Samuel Breck Parkman, Savannah, Ga.
Francis Ormond French, *Hon. Mem.; LL. B.* 1869, New York, N. Y.

1858

Alexander Agassiz, *Hon. Mem.; S. B.* 1857, and 1862; *LL. D.* 1885; *S. D.* (Hon.) Cambr. 1887, Bologna 1888; Overseer; Fellow; Cur. Mus. Comparative Zoölogy; Fellow Am. Acad.; Memb. Am. Philos. Soc.; Cor. Memb. Linnean Soc. (London), Zoöl. Soc. (London), Kön. Gesellsch. Wissensch. (Göttingen), Kön. Baier. Akad. Wissensch. (Munich), Acad. Sciences (Institut de France); For. Memb. Reale Accad. dei Lincei (Rome); Cor. Memb. Kön. Kais. Akad. Wissensch. (Vienna); For. Memb. Kön. Böhm. Gesellsch. Wissensch. (Prague); Hon. Memb. Kon. Zoolog. Genootsch. (Amsterdam), Nat. Acad. Sci., Acad. Sci. N. Y., Acad. Sci. Chicago, California Acad. Sci., Manchester (Eng.) Geol. Soc., Roy. Microscop. Soc. (London), Soc. Mexicana Hist. Nat., Soc. Phys. et d'Hist. Nat. (Geneva), Cambridge.
Gunning Samuel Bedford, *Hon. Mem.; A. B.* Columbia 1855, also *A. M.* Columbia; *LL. B.* 1859, New York, N. Y.
Josiah Bradley, *D. M'l*, Boston.
Louis Cabot, Brookline.
Benjamin William Crowninshield, *A. M.* Boston.
Robert Livingston Cutting, *Hon. Mem.* Columbia 1856, and *A. M.* Columbia; *LL. B.* 1859, New York, N. Y.

William Payne Hall, *Hon. Mem.* Boston.
John Homans, *M. D.* 1862; Fellow Am. Acad. Boston.
*Hollis Hunnewell, *L. P. C.* Boston.
WILLIAM HENRY FITZHUGH LEE, Governor of Virginia, Arlington, Va.
*James May, Petersburg, Va.
William Frederick Milton, West Roxbury.
*Daniel Chamberlain Payne, *A. M.* 1865, Boston.
John Hooper Reed, *Hon. Mem.* Boston.

1859

*Heyward Cutting, *D. M'l,* New York, N. Y.
John Chipman Gray, *A. M.; LL. B.* 1861; Story Prof. Law, Royall Prof. Law, Fellow Am. Acad. Boston.
Frederic Sears Grand d'Hauteville, *A. M.* Boston.
*Henry Hobson Richardson, *A. M.* 1872, New Orleans, La.
James Augustus Rumrill, *L. P. C.* Springfield.
*Strong Vincent, Erie, Pa.

1860

Frederick Wainwright Bradlee, *G. M'l,* Boston.
Caspar Crowninshield, *D. M'l,* Boston.
Frank Hazeltine, Philadelphia, Pa.
Francis Welles Hunnewell, *A. M.; LL. B.* 1864, Boston.
John Welles Hunnewell, *A. M.; S. B.* 1863; *L. P. C.* Boston.
*Charles Alston Pringle, Charleston, S. C.
Henry Sturgis Russell, *G. M'l,* West Roxbury.
*Robert Gould Shaw, 1873, New York, N. Y.
*Benjamin Smith Skinner, Hertford, N. C.
*Thomas Greely Stevenson, *Hon. Mem.* Boston.
*John Corlies White, New York, N. Y.
James Henry Wilson, Keene, N. H.

1861

William Hathaway Forbes, *Hon. Mem.* 1872, Milton.
*James Reeve Gould, *A. M.* 1865. New York, N. Y.
Norwood Penrose Hallowell, *D. M'l,* Philadelphia, Pa.
OLIVER WENDELL HOLMES, *LL. B.* 1866; *LL. D.*

Yale 1886; Prof. Law; Fellow Am. Acad.; Just. Supr. Court Mass. Boston.
*Edward Greely Loring, *Hon. Mem.* Boston.
John Gardner Perry, *Hon. Mem.; M. D.* 1863, Cambridge.
*Thomas Rodman Robeson, *L. P. C.* Jamaica Plain.

1862

*Copley Amory, *Hon. Mem.* Boston.
Arthur Amory, Brookline.
*Charles Boyden, Cambridge.
*Francis Lowell Gardner, Boston.
Mayo Williamson Hazeltine, *A. M.* 1866, Belfast, Me.
Henry Upham Jeffries, *D. M'l,* Boston.
John Witherspoon Labouisse, 1882, New Orleans, La.
*Herbert Cowpland Mason, Boston.
*Benjamin Crowninshield Mifflin, *L. P. C.* Boston.
Henry Parker Quincy, *A. M.* 1866; *M. D.* 1867, Dedham.
Winthrop Henry Sargent, Fishk. Land., N. Y.
*William James Temple, Albany, N. Y.

1863

Charles Walter Amory, Boston.
Robert Amory, *A. M.; M. D.* 1866; Prof. Physiol. Bowd. Coll.; Fellow Am. Acad. Brookline.
Nathan Appleton, *A. M.* Boston.
Albert Chevalier Haseltine, *L. P. C.* Philadelphia, Pa.
Amos Lawrence Mason, *M. D.* 1872; *D. M'l, G. M'l,* Boston.
James Lewis Pearce, *A. M.; Hon. Mem.* Maysville, Ky.
George Brune Shattuck, *A. M.* 1867; *M. D.* 1869; Overseer; *G. M'l,* Boston.
John Collins Warren, *M. D.* 1866; Asst. Prof. and Assoc. Prof. Surg.; Fellow Am. Acad.; *G. M'l,* Boston.
John Winthrop, *A. M.* Boston.

1864

*John Adams Blanchard, *A. M.* Boston.
Richard Codman, *A. M.* 1870; *D. M'l,* Boston.
Richard Henry Derby, *A. M.; M. D.* 1867, Boston.
John Alvarez Dillon, *A. M.; L. P. C.* St. Louis, Mo.

William Rotch Robeson, *A. M.; LL. B.* 1868, Cambridge.
William Phillips Walley, *A. M.* 1872; *LL. B.* 1866, Boston.

1865

James Read Chadwick, *A. M.; M. D.* 1871, Boston.
*Jabez Silas Holmes, *A. M.* New York, N. Y.
Walter Hunnewell, 1875, Boston.
George Harrison Mifflin, *L. P. C.* Boston.
William Lawrence Tucker, *A. M.; LL. B.* 1875; *D. M'l,* Boston.

1866

Samuel Appleton Browne Abbott, *A. M.* 1872, Boston.
Charles Holder Borden Bowen, Providence, R. I.
*Edward Henry Clark, 1867; *LL. B.* Columbia 1872, St. Louis, Mo.
Frederic Crowninshield, Boston.
Thomas Dwight, 1872; *M. D.* 1867; *LL. D.* Georgetown (D. C.) 1889; Instr. Histol.; Instr. Topogr. Anat.; Parkman Prof. Anat.; Prof. Anat. Bowd. Coll.; Fellow Am. Acad.; Memb. Acad. Philos.-Med. S. Thomae Aquin. (Rome) Boston.
James Murray Forbes, *Hon. Mem.* Milton.
Richard Cranch Greenleaf, *M. D.* 1870, Boston.
Charles Heber McBurney, *A. M.; M. D.* Columbia 1869, Roxbury.
*George Gordon Meade, *Hon. Mem.*, Maj. Gen. U. S. A. Philadelphia, Pa.
Thomas Sargeant Perry, *A. M.;* Tutor; *L. P. C.* Philadelphia, Pa.
William George Tiffany, Baltimore, Md.
George Dudley Welles, *D. M'l,* Boston.

1867

Thomas Sprague Edmands, *D. M'l,* Newton.
*William Homer, *L. P. C.* Boston.
Arthur L. Jones, *A. M.; LL. B.* 1869, Cambridge.
*William Rollins Tappan, *A. M.* 1872, Boston.
Frederick Tudor, Boston.

1868

Robert Apthorp Boit,	Boston.
Augustus George Bullock, *A. M.; L. P. C.*	Worcester.
Dawes Eliot Furness, *A. M.; D. M'l,*	Philadelphia, Pa.
Arthur Hunnewell,	Boston.
*Edward Jackson Holmes, *Hon. Mem.; LL. B.* 1869,	Boston.
Charles Taylor Lovering, *A. M.; LL. B.* 1870; *Tr.*	Boston.
Thomas Motley, *Hon. Mem.*	Boston.
William Whitlock Richards, *A. M.* 1872,	New York, N. Y.
Frederick Cheever Shattuck, *A. M.* 1872; *M. D.* 1873; Jackson Prof. Clin. Med.; *G. M'l,*	Boston.
Leverett Saltonstall Tuckerman, *A. M.; LL. B.* 1871,	Salem.

1869

Francis Henry Appleton, *A. M.; D. M'l,*	Boston.
Franklin Bartlett, *A. M.; LL. B.* Columbia 1873; *Ph. D.* and *A. M.* (*Hist.*) 1873; *L. P. C.*	New York, N. Y.
*Dudley Pickman Rogers, *A. M.*	Salem.

1870

Brooks Adams,	Quincy.
George Huntington Adams,	Jacksonville, Ill.
John Edwin Hill,	Stoneham.
Francis Key Pendleton, *LL. B.* 1875,	Cincinnati, O.
Alfred Rodman, *LL. B.* Boston Univ. 1879,	Boston.
Lucius Manlius Sargent, *LL. B.* 1875,	Boston.
*Stephen Van Rensselaer Thayer, *D. M'l,*	Boston.
William Austin Wadsworth, *L. P. C.*	Geneseo, N. Y.

1871

Francis Inman Amory, *LL. B.* 1875,	Boston.
William Sturgis Bigelow, *M. D.* 1874,	Boston.
Dudley Hall Bradlee,	Boston.
Jesse Brown,	Washington, D. C.
Walter Clifford, *LL. B.* 1875,	New Bedford.
Horatio Appleton Lamb,	Boston.
HENRY CABOT LODGE, *LL. B.* 1874; *Ph. D.*	

(*Hist.*) 1876; Overseer; Memb. Mass. Hist. Soc.; Fellow Am. Acad.; *M. C.* Boston.
James Selden McCobb, Portland, Me.
*James Rownd Morris, Baltimore, Md.
James Patterson Scott, *D. M'l,* Philadelphia, Pa.
*William Lawrence Sprague, *M. D.* 1881, Boston.
Nathaniel Thayer, *Tr.* Boston.
William Tudor, *L. P. C.* Boston.

1872

PERRY BELMONT, *LL. B.* Columbia; *M. C.*; U. S. Min. Plen. Spain; Chev. Légion d'Honneur, New York, N. Y.
*Richard Augustine Gambrill, *LL. B.* 1876; *L. P. C.* Baltimore, Md.
Lawrence Dana Rumsey, Buffalo, N. Y.
Charles Howland Russell, *LL. B.* Columbia 1874, New York, N. Y.
*Robert Shaw Russell, Boston.
Alanson Tucker, *D. M'l,* Boston.
*Francis Minot Weld, Boston.
George Webb West, *M. D.* 1880, Salem.

1873

John Bryant, *M. D.* 1878, Boston.
Joshua Cleaves Dodge, *L. P. C.* Boston.
Frederick Getman Fincke, *LL. B.* Columbia 1875; *D. M'l,* New York, N. Y.
Dudley Leavitt Pickman, Boston.

1874

August Belmont, New York, N. Y.
William Appleton Burnham, *Tr.* Boston.
Louis Crawford Clark, New York, N. Y.
*Arthur Clifford, *M. D.* Dart. 1878, New Bedford.
Edgar Mora Davison, New York, N. Y.
James Lawrence, *D. M'l,* Boston.
Henry Sanford Mudge, 1876, Boston.
Edward Gould Peters, Boston.
George Saltonstall Silsbee, *Hon. Mem.* Salem.
Charles Sanders Tuckerman, *L. P. C.* Salem.

1875

Francis Randall Appleton, *LL. B.* Columbia 1877; *D. M'l*, New York, N. Y.
Sidney Williams Burgess, Boston.
Henry Sargent Hunnewell, Boston.
*Abbott Lawrence, *LL. B.* 1877, Boston.
Frederick Richard Sears, Boston.
Francis Shaw, *L. P. C.* Boston.
Samuel Gray Ward, New York, N. Y.
Samuel Dennis Warren, *LL. B.* 1877; *A. M.* 1878, Boston.

1876

Harcourt Amory, Brookline.
Thomas Trueman Gaff, Cincinnati, O.
Edward Cunningham Hall, *Hon. Mem.* Kingston.
Charles Isham, *L. P. C.* New York, N. Y.
Samuel Sherwood, *LL. B.* Columbia 1878; *D. M'l*, New York, N. Y.

1877

Frederic Tilden Brown, 1878; *M. D.* Columbia 1880, New York, N. Y.
Nathaniel Curtis, Boston.
Arthur Briggs Denny, Boston.
Truman Heminway, *LL. B.* Columbia 1880; *L. P. C.* New Rochelle, N. Y.
*Edwin Hayden Herrick, *LL. B.* Columbia 1879, New York, N. Y.
Henry Thomas Kidder, Boston.
Edward Sandford Martin, Auburn, N. Y.
George Barnewell Ogden, New York, N. Y
Augustus Clifford Tower, Lexington.
*Henry Upham, 1878; *D. M'l*, Boston.
*John Russell Wright, Boston.

1878

Hubert Engelbert Teschemacher, San Francisco, Cal.
Emmons Blaine, *L. P. C.* Augusta, Me.
Philip Van Rensselaer Ely, Marquette, Mich.
Edwin Denison Morgan, New York, N. Y.
James Parker, *D. M'l*, Boston.
John Homans, *M. D.* 1882, *Hon. Mem.* Boston.

DINING HALL—NEW CLUB

1879

William Bayard Van Rensselaer,	Albany, N. Y.
Otho Holland Williams, *D. M'l,*	Baltimore, Md.
James Anderson Wright,	Philadelphia, Pa.
Charles Franklin Sprague, 1880; *L. P. C.*	Boston.
John Templeton Bowen, *M. D.* 1884,	Boston.
Herman Stewart LeRoy,	New York, N. Y.
Walter Trimble, *LL. B.* Columbia 1881,	New York, N. Y.
Edmund Lincoln Baylies, *LL. B.* 1882 and Columbia 1882,	New York, N. Y.
Francis McLennan, *Hon. Mem.*	Montreal, Ca.

1880

George Griswold,	New York, N. Y.
Charles Morgan,	New York, N. Y.
Francis Peabody, *Hon. Mem.*	Salem.
Theodore Roosevelt, *L. P. C.*	New York, N. Y.
Richard Middlecott Saltonstall, *Tr.*	Chestnut Hill.
Henry Russell Shaw, *D. M'l,*	Boston.
John Sever Tebbits,	Boston.
Richard Trimble,	New York, N. Y.
Christopher Minot Weld,	Boston.

1881

Edward Deshon Brandegee,	Utica, N. Y.
William Brewster,	Boston.
Dudley Bowditch Fay,	Boston.
Samuel Hammond, Jr.	Boston.
William York Peters,	Boston.
Rodman Paul Snelling,	Boston.
Richard Sprague, *L. C. P.; M. D.* 1887,	Boston.
George Phinehas Upham, *D. M'l,*	Boston.
Samuel Hammond, *Hon. Mem.*	Boston.

1882

James Williams Bowen,	Boston.
Charles Denston Dickey, *L. P. C.*	New York, N. Y.
Frederick Ware Emerson,	Newton.

Woodbury Kane, *D. M'l,*	New York, N. Y.
Robert Treat Paine,	Boston.
Endicott Peabody, Hon. Mem.	Salem.
Henry Dwight Sedgwick,	Stockbridge.
Stephen Van Rensselaer Townsend,	Albany, N. Y.
Guy Waring,	Newport, R. I.
Owen Wister, *LL. B.* and *A. M.* 1888,	Philadelphia, Pa.

1883

Henry Bromfield Cabot, *LL. B.* 1887,	Boston.
Henry Grafton Chapman,	New York, N. Y.
Charles Pelham Curtis, *D. M'l,*	Boston.
William Otis Edmands,	Newton.
Charles Mifflin Hammond,	New London, Conn.
William Pratt Lyman,	Boston.
Joseph Lee, *LL. B.* and *A. M.* 1887,	Boston.
Henry Francis Sears, *A. M.* 1888; *M. D.* 1887; *L. P. C.*	Boston.
Richard Dudley Sears,	Boston.

1884

George Russell Agassiz,	Cambridge.
Randolph Morgan Appleton,	New York, N. Y.
Walter Cabot Baylies, *L. P. C.*	New York, N. Y.
Louis Alexander Biddle,	Philadelphia, Pa.
William Sohier Bryant, *M. D.* and *A. M.* 1888,	Boston.
John Jay Chapman,	New York, N. Y.
Frank Haven Clark, *M. D.* 1888,	Detroit, Mich.
Robert Patterson Perkins, *D. M'l,*	New York, N. Y.
Herbert Daniel Robbins,	Brooklyn, N. Y.
John Allison White.	Williamsport, Pa.

1885

Royal Phelps Carroll,	Howard Co., Md.
Winthrop Astor Chanler, *D. M'l,*	New York, N. Y.
Hamilton Rowan Curtis,	Boston.
Amos Tuck French, *L. P. C.*	New York, N. Y.
John Lawrence,	Boston.
Robert Latimer McCook,	Steubenville, O.
John Hawks Noble,	Cambridge.
Egerton Leigh Winthrop, *LL. B.* Columbia 1887,	New York, N. Y.

1886

Oliver Ames, *D. M'l*,	North Easton.
*Raymond Rodgers Belmont,	New York, N. Y.
Oliver William Bird,	New York, N. Y.
David Crawford Clark,	New York, N. Y.
Frank Ravenel Frost,	Charleston, S. C.
Francis Stanley Parker,	Nahant.
George Lee Peabody,	Salem.
William Reynolds Wilson, *M. D.* 1888; *L. P. C.*	Philadelphia, Pa.
Grenville Lindall Winthrop, *LL. B.* 1889,	New York, N. Y.

1887

Charles Carroll,	Howard Co., Md.
Elisha Flagg,	Boston.
Gordon Dexter, *L. P. C.*	Boston.
Franklin Remington, *D. M'l*,	Cazenovia, N. Y.
John Linzee Snelling,	Boston.
Arthur William Wheelwright,	Boston.

1888

Copley Amory,	Boston.
James Waldingfield Appleton, *D. M'l*,	New York, N. Y.
Charles Bohlen, *L. P. C.*	Philadelphia, Pa.
John Hunter Sedgwick,	New York, N. Y.
John Stansbury Tooker,	Newport, R. I.
John Walter Wood,	South Orange, N. J.

1889

Maximilian Agassiz,	Cambridge.
Henry Reginald Astor Carey,	New York, N. Y.
Gerald Hull Gray,	New York, N. Y.
James Brown Markoe,	Philadelphia, Pa.
Lewis Henry Morgan, *D. M'l*,	Washington, D. C.
George H. Norman,	Newport, R. I.
George Blair Painter, *L. P. C.*	Pittsburgh, Pa.
Philip Leverett Saltonstall,	Boston.
Herbert Mason Sears,	Boston.
Philip Shelton Sears,	Boston.
James Wheatland Smith,	Salem.

1890

Arthur Amory,	Boston.
Thomas Stevenson Bradlee,	Boston.
William Astor Chanler,	New York, N. Y.
Robert Ives Crocker,	New York, N. Y.
Hollis Horatio Hunnewell, *L. P. C.*	Boston.
Guy Norman,	Newport, R. I.
Richard Fay Parker, *D. Ml,*	Boston.

N. B. These names of the residences of Members in the Catalogue have been taken from the old records; and as it has been found impossible to correct them all in conformity with the changes which have since been made, they have been generally suffered to remain as first recorded. This may account for some misstatements in the present residences of members.

Members are urgently requested to notify the librarian of any errors they may discover in the Catalogue.

IMMEDIATE MEMBERS

1891

William Amory,	Longwood.
Francis Reginald Bangs,	Boston.
Lawrence Brooks, *L. P. C.*	Boston.
John Watson Lawrence,	New York, N. Y.
Nicholas Longworth, *D. M'l,*	Cincinnati, Ohio.
Thomas Nelson Perkins,	Milton.
Frederic Bayard Winthrop,	New York, N. Y.

1892

Rudolphe Louis Agassiz,	Cambridge.
Ingersoll Amory, Treasurer,	Boston.
Samuel Thompson Chase, *C.* and *R. S. P. C.*	Chicago, Ill.
Morton Jackson Henry,	Philadelphia, Pa.
Francis Skinner,	Boston.
Frederic Newell Watriss,	Chicago, Ill.

1893

Columbus Calvert Baldwin,	New York, N. Y.
James Abercrombie Burden,	Troy, N. Y.
George Richmond Fearing,	Newport, R. I.
Louis Adams Frothingham,	Boston.

SUMMARY

Total number of members down to date		1211
Deceased		834
Total number of members living		377
Immediate members	17	
Honorary members	360	
Total	377	

INDEX

INDEX

OF THE

PORCELLIAN CATALOGUE

*1836 John William Tudor
*1852 John Sylvester

Gardner
*1793 Francis
*1821 John Lowell
*1829 George
*1847 Joseph Peabody
*1862 Francis Lowell

Garrow
*1825 William M.

Gates
1835 Charles Horatio

Gay
*1810 George
*1823 Martin

Geyer
*1794 Thomas

Gibbes
*1812 Allston
*1813 Washington
*1824 Benjamin S.

Gilchrist
*1828 John James

Gilman
*1818 Joseph
*1819 Samuel Taylor

Gilmore
*1828 Robert

Gordon
*1806 William

Gorham
*1795 Benjamin
*1801 John
*1821 David Wood
*1831 William Cabot
*1832 John Warren

Gould
*1861 James Reeve

Gourdin
*1821 John Gaillard Keith
*1821 Robert Marion

Grant
1828 Patrick

Gratz
*1827 Simon

Gray
*1809 Francis Calley
*1811 John Chipman
*1819 Horace
*1824 John Henry
1829 William
*1833 Henry Yancey
1836 John Thompson
1859 John Chipman
1889 Gerald Hull

Greene
*1800 David Ireland
*1812 Benjamin David
*1828 John Singleton Copley

Greenleaf
1866 Richard Cranch

Greenough
*1805 David Stoddard
1837 William Whitwell
*1842 James

Griswold
1880 George

Guild
*1804 Benjamin

Habersham
*1831 Robert
1836 William Neyle
1845 John Rae
*1851 Alexander Telfair

Hall
*1820 David Priestly
1856 Rowland Minturn
1858 William Payne
1876 Edward Cunningham

Hallowell
1861 Norwood Penrose

Halyburton
*1823 James Dandridge

Hamilton
*1798 John

Hammond
1881 Samuel
1881 Samuel, Jr.
1883 Charles Mifflin

Harper
*1823 Charles Carroll

Harris
*1802 Richard Devens
*1807 William Coffin
*1830 Benjamin Gwinn
*1831 Charles

Haseltine
1854 William Stanley
1860 Frank
1863 Albert Chevalier

Haskell
*1799 Elnathan
*1823 Charles Thompson

Haslett
*1819 John

Hathaway
*1818 Nathaniel
1849 Francis
1850 Horatio

Hauteville, D'
1859 Frederic Sears Grand

Haven
*1807 Nathaniel Appleton
*1813 John Appleton
*1820 Alfred Woodward

Hazeltine
1862 Mayo Williamson

Heard
*1795 John
*1812 George Washington
1847 Augustine

Heath
*1840 John Francis
*1847 Roscoe Briggs

Hedge
*1820 Isaac Lothrop

Heminway
1877 Truman

Henderson
*1815 Arthur Moseley

Henry
1892 Morton Jackson

Henshaw
*1808 John H.

Heriot
*1815 William Francis

Herrick
*1877 Edward Hayden

Heyward
*1806 James
*1818 Joshua Henshaw
*1838 James Barnwell
*1838 William Henry

Hichborn
*1816 Doddridge Crocker

Higginson
1833 Waldo

Hildreth
*1805 Hosea
*1837 Samuel Tenney

Hill
1870 John Edwin

Hobson
*1848 John David

Holley
*1813 Orville Luther

Holmes
1829 Oliver Wendell
*1837 Christopher Columbus
1861 Oliver Wendell
*1865 Jabez Silas
1868 Edward Jackson

Homans
*1812 John
1858 John
1878 John

Homer
*1812 George
*1867 William

Hook
*1798 Moses
*1827 Edward William

Hooper
*1811 Robert
*1815 William
*1819 Nathaniel Leech
*1830 Robert William

Hosmer
*1800 Rufus

Howe
*1810 Isaac Reddington
*1815 Appleton
*1852 William Edward

Hubbard
*1821 George Johonnot
*1837 Henry
*1840 Nathaniel Dean

Huger
*1813 Benjamin
*1837 Joseph Alston

Hulbert
*1795 John Whitefield

Hull
*1805 Abraham Fuller

Hunnewell
*1858 Hollis
1860 Francis Welles
1860 John Welles
1865 Walter
1868 Arthur
1875 Henry Sargent
1890 Hollis Horatio

Hunt
*1795 Ebenezer
*1826 Charles J.
*1844 William Morris
*1845 Jonathan
1856 Leavitt

Huntington
*1822 Charles Phelps

Hurd
*1806 Isaac

Inches
*1792 Henderson
*1831 Herman Brimmer

Ingersoll
*1815 George Goldthwait

Ingraham
*1809 Daniel Greenleaf
Isham
1876 Charles
Izard
*1824 Walter

Jackson
*1793 Charles
*1796 James
*1828 James
*1833 Charles
1849 Edward
Jarvis
*1800 Leonard
Jeffries
1854 Benjamin Joy
*1856 Edward Payson
1862 Henry Upham
Jenkins
*1829 Solomon Martin
Jewett
*1830 Isaac Appleton
Johnston
*1849 Henry Elliott
1849 Josiah Lee
Jones
*1793 William
*1806 Thomas Morton
*1816 John Coffin
*1835 Daniel
1867 Arthur Earle
Jouve
*1826 Adolphus Peter
*1826 George Caspar
Joy
*1797 John
*1833 John

Kane
1882 Woodbury
Keating
*1814 Charles
Kendall
*1810 Joseph Gowing
Kent
*1795 Amos
*1801 Moody
Kerr
*1830 John Bozman
Kidder
1877 Henry Thomas
Kimball
*1804 Leonard
*1814 Edmund
King
*1802 John
*1807 John Glen
Kingsbury
*1827 William Bradbury
Kinloch
*1810 Frederick
Kirkland
*1803 Samuel
Kittredge
*1795 John
Knapp
*1800 John
Kollock
*1813 Phineas Miller

La Beaume
*1842 Chauvet Edmund
Labouisse
1862 John Witherspoon
Labranche
*1834 Drausin Balthazar
*1835 Nemèse Harmogène
*1839 Romuald
Ladd
*1797 William
Lamb
1871 Horatio Appleton
Lane
1846 George Martin
Latham
*1818 Bela
Law
*1804 John
*1819 Edward Ellenborough
Lawrence
*1834 Rufus Bigelow
*1835 Amos Adams
*1840 James
*1846 Timothy Bigelow
1849 Abbott
1874 James
*1875 Abbott
1885 John
1891 John Watson
Lazarus
*1829 Washington
Lee
*1798 Thomas
*1809 John
*1819 Charles Carter
*1827 Alfred
*1843 Francis L.
1858 William Henry Fitzhugh
1883 Joseph

Leonard
*1815 Levi Washburn

LeRoy
1879 Herman Stewart

Lewis
*1819 Winslow

Lincoln
*1800 Isaac
*1806 Benjamin
*1807 James Otis

Lloyd
*1824 Horatio Nelson

Lodge
1871 Henry Cabot

Longfellow
*1798 Stephen

Longworth
1891 Nicholas

Lord
*1798 Nathaniel

Loring
*1828 Francis Caleb
*1861 Edward Greely

Lothrop
*1825 Samuel Kirkland

Lovering
1868 Charles Taylor

Lowell
*1793 Francis Cabot
*1800 Charles
*1821 Francis Cabot
*1822 Edward Jackson
*1826 Charles Russell
1838 James Russell
*1850 George Gardner

Lowndes
*1824 Thomas

Lyman
*1806 George Williams
*1810 Theodore
*1817 Wyllys
*1819 Charles
*1830 Joseph
1842 George Theodore
*1855 Charles Frederick
1855 Theodore
1883 William Pratt

Lyon
*1821 Samuel Hall

Macfarland
*1849 James Edward

Mackenzie
*1847 Colin

Manigault
*1821 Joseph
*1825 Charles D.
*1825 Peter

Markoe
1889 James Brown

Marshall
*1826 Edward Carrington

Martin
*1814 James G.
1877 Edward Sandford

Mason
*1811 William Powell
*1815 Jonathan
1856 William Powell
*1862 Herbert Cowpland
1863 Amos Lawrence

May
*1810 George Washington
*1817 Samuel Joseph
1829 Samuel
*1858 James

McBurney
1866 Charles Heber

McCobb
1871 James Selden

McCollock
*1818 Thomas

McCook
1885 Robert Latimer

McKean
*1794 Joseph
*1828 Henry Swasey
*1831 John George

McLaughlin
*1838 Thomas

McLennan
1879 Francis

Meade
*1866 George Gordon

Means
*1808 Robert

Mellen
*1814 John Wendell
*1818 Grenville

Meredith
*1827 George Augustus

Merrick
*1814 Pliny

Middleton
*1814 Arthur

Mifflin
*1862 Benjamin Crowninshield
1865 George Harrison

Miller
*1825 William
Milliken
*1829 Edward Patrick
Milton
1858 William Frederick
Minge
1823 David
Minot
*1802 William
1836 William
Mitchell
*1802 Thomas Rothmahler
*1817 Sylvanus Lazell
*1822 Richard Bennet Granger
Monroe
*1800 Israel
Moore
*1806 Abraham
*1828 Eugene Thomas Whittell
*1839 Thomas Johnson
Morey
*1811 George
Morgan
*1826 William H.
1878 Edwin Denison
1880 Charles
1889 Lewis Henry
Morrell
*1847 Charles Henry
Morris
*1818 Richard
*1822 George M.
*1854 Gerard Walton
*1871 James Rownd
Morse
*1829 Isaac Edward
Motley
*1831 John Lothrop
1868 Thomas
Motte
*1821 Mellish Irving
*1832 Rhett Jacob
Moulton
*1815 William H.
Mudge
1874 Henry Sanford
Murdoch
*1828 Charles Tracy
Murray
*1826 James L.
Myers
*1817 Samuel H.
Neil
1847 William Allen
Newell
*1802 Timothy
Newman
*1816 Samuel Phillips
Neyle
*1821 Henry Manley
Nichols
1842 Benjamin White
Nicholson
*1803 Robert
Noble
1885 John Hawks
Norman
1889 George H.
1890 Guy
North
*1825 John G.
*1826 Edward

Ogden
1877 George Barnewell
Oliver
*1795 Francis Johonnot
*1806 Daniel
*1809 Nathaniel Kemble Greenwood
*1833 Francis Eben
Orne
*1815 Joseph
*1841 William Henry
Osborn
*1820 George Barber
Osgood
*1806 Benjamin Binney
*1811 Robert Hawkins
*1815 Gayton Pickman
Otis
*1811 Harrison Gray
*1821 William Foster
*1825 Allyne

Page
*1809 William Putnam
Paine
*1792 Robert Treat
*1802 Thomas
*1813 Martyn
*1820 Charles
*1827 Charles Cushing
1882 Robert Treat
Painter
1889 George Blair
Palfrey
*1815 John Gorham

Park
*1808 John

Parker
1835 Charles Henry
1878 James
1886 Francis Stanley
1890 Richard Fay

Parkman
*1813 Daniel
*1832 John
*1834 Samuel
*1857 Samuel Breck

Parks
*1813 Gorham

Parsons
*1815 Theophilus
*1818 William

Payne
*1824 William Edward
*1858 Daniel Chamberlain

Payson
*1817 John Larkin
*1819 Phillips

Peabody
*1816 Joseph Augustus
*1816 Oliver William Bourn
*1816 William Bourn Oliver
1823 George
1852 George Augustus
1880 Francis
1882 Endicott
1886 George Lee

Pearce
1863 James Lewis

Pearson
*1816 Henry Bromfield

Peirce
*1808 Henry
*1829 Benjamin
*1833 Charles Henry

Pendleton
1870 Frank Key

Penniman
*1822 Henry Harding

Percy
*1825 Robert Dow

Perkins
*1809 James
*1811 Thomas
1827 William Powell
1841 Edward Newton
*1843 Charles Callahan
1843 Thomas Handasyde
*1851 Augustus Thorndike
1884 Robert Patterson
1891 Thomas Nelson

Perry
*1816 Samuel
1861 John Gardner
1866 Thomas Sargeant

Peters
1874 Edward Gould
1881 William York

Phillips
*1795 John
*1819 Stephen Clarendon
*1826 John Charles
*1828 William
*1829 George William
*1831 Wendell
*1836 Grenville Tudor
1842 Stephen Henry
1855 Willard Quincy

Pickering
*1796 John
*1799 Timothy

Pickman
*1815 Hasket Derby
1873 Dudley Leavitt

Pinckney
*1808 Charles Cotesworth

Pomeroy
1853 Charles Coolidge

Pope
*1821 William H.

Porter
*1814 Jonathan

Pratt
*1821 George Williams
*1824 William
1852 Edward Ellerton

Prescott
*1814 William Hickling
*1825 Edward Goldsborough

Preston
*1838 William

Prince
*1800 John

Pringle
*1813 Robert
*1838 Benjamin Gardner
1845 Edward J.
*1860 Charles Alston

Putnam
*1800 Aaron Hall
*1824 Charles Gideon

Quash
*1814 Francis Dallas

Quincy
*1827 Edmund
1862 Henry Parker

Schuyler
*1813 John
*1817 Robert
*1820 Stephen
*1827 William

Scollay
*1804 William
*1810 John

Scott
1871 James Patterson

Sears
*1807 David
*1842 David
1843 Frederick Richard
1852 Knyvett Winthrop
1875 Frederick Richard
1883 Henry Francis
1883 Richard Dudley
1889 Herbert Mason
1889 Philip Shelton

Seaton
*1837 Joseph Gales

Seaver
*1822 Norman

Sedgwick
*1813 Theodore
*1830 Theodore
*1846 Winslow Ellery
1882 Henry Dwight
1888 John Hunter

Sever
*1818 Winslow Warren

Sewall
*1803 William Bartlett
*1815 Edmund Quincy

Shaler
*1827 Nathaniel Burger

Shattuck
1831 George Cheyne
1863 George Brune
1868 Frederick Cheever

Shaw
*1805 Charles
*1832 Samuel Parkman
*1840 Joseph Coolidge
1845 Quincy Adams
*1860 Robert Gould
1875 Francis
1880 Henry Russell

Sheafe
*1798 George
*1817 Oliver
*1825 George
*1829 James Edward

Sheldon
1842 Frederick

Sheppard
*1808 John Hannibal

Sherwood
1876 Samuel

Sigourney
*1809 William Parsons

Silsbee
*1824 Nathaniel
*1831 Francis Henry
*1832 John Boardman
1852 Nathaniel Devereux
1874 George Saltonstall

Skinner
*1860 Benjamin Smith
1892 Francis

Smith
*1805 Robert
*1807 William
*1808 Samuel Emerson
*1811 Edwin
*1811 William
*1820 William Rufus
*1824 Calvin Stephen
*1824 Josiah
1889 James Wheatland

Snead
*1839 Thomas

Snelling
1819 George Henry
1881 Rodman Paul
1887 John Linzee

Snow
*1830 Theodore William

Sohier
*1852 George Brimmer

Soley
*1817 Samuel

Spear
*1817 Samuel Perkins

Spooner
*1813 William Jones

Sprague
*1799 Samuel John
*1804 Joseph E.
*1812 Peleg
*1871 William Lawrence
1879 Charles Franklin
1881 Richard

Spring
*1812 Marshall Binney

Stephens
*1810 Thomas

Steuart
*1820 William M.

Stevenson
*1816 Jonathan
*1860 Thomas Greely

Stiles
*1830 William Henry

Randolph
*1802 Richard Kidder
Read
*1820 William George
*1836 John Harleston
Reed
*1821 Benjamin Tyler
1858 John Hooper
Relf
*1824 Daniel Clark
Remington
1887 Franklin
Renshaw
1854 Robert Aloysius
Revere
*1852 Paul Joseph
Reynolds
*1811 Edward
Rice
*1803 Caleb
*1842 George Edward
1856 Francis Blake
Richards
*1822 John Holbrook
1868 William Whitlock
Richardson
*1799 Luther
*1825 John Hancock
*1859 Henry Hobson
Ridgely
*1850 Charles
Ritchie
1845 Harrison
Rives
*1847 William Cabell
Robbins
*1812 Edward Hutchinson
*1815 Chandler
*1829 Chandler
1884 Herbert Daniel
Robertson
*1814 Elbridge B.
*1818 Edward
Robeson
*1861 Thomas Rodman
1864 William Rotch
Robinson
*1842 Samuel Couch
Rodman
*1842 Alfred
*1842 William Logan
1846 Thomas R.
1870 Alfred
Rogers
*1820 John
*1822 Henry Bromfield
*1843 William Crowninshield
*1869 Dudley Pickman
Roosevelt
1827 William Henry
*1853 James Noon
1880 Theodore
Rose
*1813 James
Rotch
*1838 Benjamin Smith
1838 William James
*1841 Francis Morgan
Rowe
1827 James Gillespie
Rumrill
1859 James Augustus
Rumsey
1872 Lawrence Dana
Rundlet
*1825 Edward
Russell
*1796 John
*1807 William W.
*1811 James
1860 Henry Sturgis
1872 Charles Howland
*1872 Robert Shaw
Rutledge
*1808 Hugh
*1811 John
*1835 Thomas Pinckney

Saltonstall
*1802 Leverett
1844 Leverett
1880 Richard Middlecott
1889 Philip Leverett
Sargent
*1803 Winthrop
*1827 John Turner
*1829 Howard
*1830 Henry Winthrop
1830 John Osborne
*1834 John Turner Welles
1862 Winthrop Henry
1870 Lucius Manlius
Saul
*1829 Benjamin Morgan
Savage
*1803 James
*1807 Arthur
*1827 James
Sawyer
*1798 Artemas
Schley
*1855 Samuel Ringgold

Stilwell
1839 Richard Cleveland
Stone
*1844 Joshua Clapp
Storrow
*1808 Samuel M. A.
1829 Charles Storer
Story
*1798 Joseph
1838 William Wetmore
Stout
*1822 Henry
Strong
*1810 Edward
Stuart
*1801 George O'Kill
Sturges
*1795 Josiah
Sturgis
*1823 Russell
*1829 William Watson
Sullivan
*1798 Richard
*1801 George
*1801 William Bant
*1817 Thomas Russell
*1822 James
*1830 James Swan
*1831 John T. S.
Sumner
*1830 Charles
Swett
*1829 William Gray

Taliaferro
1823 Warner T.
Tappan
*1867 William Rollins
Tarbell
1828 John Parker
Tayloe
*1815 Benjamin Ogle
*1823 Edward Thornton
Taylor
*1803 John Man
*1828 Charles Joseph
Tebbits
1880 John Sever
Temple
*1832 Henry Waring Latane
*1862 William James
Teschemacher
1878 Hubert Engelbert
Thacher
*1796 Peter Oxenbridge
*1804 Samuel Hooper
*1832 Joseph Stevens Buckminster
*1834 William Vincent
Thatcher
*1798 Ebenezer
Thayer
*1798 Gideon Latimer
*1870 Stephen Van Rensselaer
1871 Nathaniel
Thomas
*1807 William
*1822 Alexander
Thompson
*1813 Henry
*1831 Abraham Rand
Thorndike
*1808 George
*1813 William
*1816 Augustus
1848 James Steuart
1852 Samuel Lothrop
1854 Charles
*1854 William
Thwing
*1837 Supply Clapp
Tiffany
*1843 Osmond
1845 William Shaw
*1848 George Peabody
1866 William George
Tilghman
*1805 Tench
*1831 Charles Henry
Titcomb
*1801 William Starkey
*1804 Moses
Tooker
1888 John Stansbury
Toppan
*1796 Edmund
Torrey
*1808 John
*1822 Ebenezer
Tower
*1830 Charlemagne
1877 Augustus Clifford
Townsend
1882 Stephen Van Rensselaer
Trapier
*1825 Paul
Trask
*1794 Israel Eliot
Trevett
*1804 Samuel Russell

Trimble
1879 Walter
1880 Richard

Tucker
*1820 Gideon
*1824 Charles Church Chandler
*1832 Alanson
1865 William Lawrence
1872 Alanson

Tuckerman
*1837 John Francis
1868 Leverett Saltonstall
1874 Charles Sanders

Tudor
*1796 William
*1800 John Henry
*1810 Henry James
*1824 Henry Samuel
1867 Frederick
*1871 William

Tufts
*1794 Hall

Turnbull
*1797 Robert
*1821 Andrew

Turner
*1826 George Franklin

Upham
*1795 Joshua
*1819 Henry
*1821 Charles Wentworth
*1877 Henry
1881 George Phinehas

Van Rensselaer
1879 William Bayard

Vincent
*1859 Strong

Wadsworth
*1848 Alexander Scammell
1870 William Austin

Waight
*1818 Robert

Wainwright
*1812 Jonathan Mayhew

Walker
*1814 James
*1814 Julius Henry
*1818 Charles
*1825 George Augustus Beverly
*1849 John Stewart

Walley
1864 William Phillips

Walter
*1797 Arthur M.

Ward
*1809 Samuel Dexter
*1816 Henry Artemas
*1829 Joshua Holyoke
1836 Samuel Gray
*1843 George Cabot
1875 Samuel Gray

Ware
*1813 John
*1816 William

Waring
1882 Guy

Warner
*1815 William Augustus

Warren
*1800 Ebenezer Tucker
*1813 Henry
*1813 Winslow
*1815 Pelham Winslow
*1817 Charles Henry
*1832 James Sullivan
1863 John Collins
1875 Samuel Dennis

Washburn
*1816 William Rounsville Peirce

Watriss
1892 Frederic Newell

Watson
*1815 John Lee
*1820 Adolphus Eugene

Wayne
*1834 Henry Constantine

Webster
*1833 Fletcher

Welch
1833 Charles Alfred
*1840 Edward Holker

Weld
*1826 Stephen Minot
*1872 Francis Minot
1880 Christopher Minot

Welles
*1796 Samuel
*1800 Benjamin
*1827 Arnold Francis
1866 George Derby

Wellford
*1828 William Nelson

Welsh
*1798 Thomas

West
*1807 Nathaniel
*1808 David
1872 George Webb

Weston
*1829 Ezra

Wetmore
*1797 William
Wheatland
1844 Stephen Goodhue
Wheelwright
*1824 William Wilson
*1834 Charles Henry
1844 Edward
1847 Andrew Cunningham
1887 Arthur William
White
1860 John Corlies
1884 John Allison
Whitman
*1846 Bernard Crosby
Whitney
1828 Benjamin Duick
*1846 Henry Austin
Wickham
*1824 John H.
Wickliffe
*1834 Robert
Wigglesworth
*1831 Samuel
Wikoff
*1822 Daniel
Willard
*1816 Joseph
Williams
*1797 John Shirley
*1818 Robert Breck Garven
*1820 Francis Henry
*1830 Joseph Barney
1834 Joseph Hartwell
*1837 Edward Pinckney
*1837 William Pinckney
1879 Otho Holland
Willing
*1825 Charles
Willis
*1813 William
Williston
*1799 Joseph
Wilson
1860 James Henry
1886 William Reynolds
Wingate
*1796 George
Winthrop
*1817 Francis William
*1825 George Edward
1828 Robert Charles
1854 Robert Charles
1856 Thomas Lindall
1863 John
1885 Egerton Leigh
1886 Grenville Lindall
1891 Frederic Bayard
Wister
1882 Owen
Wood
*1814 David
1888 John Walter
Wright
*1877 John Russell
1879 James Anderson
Wyeth
1854 Leonard Jarvis
Wyman
*1799 Rufus

Yates
*1822 William